Maharana Sanga, The Hindupat

THE LAST GREAT LEADER OF THE RAJPUT RACE

Maharana Sanga, *The Hindupat*

THE LAST GREAT LEADER OF THE RAJPUT RACE.

BY

HAR BILAS SARDA

GYAN

Published by

Gyan Publishing House
5, Ansari Road
Daryaganj, New Delhi-110002
Phone: 011-47034999, 9811692060
E-mail: books@gyanbooks.com

Distribution Network
gyanbooks.com
India, USA, Canada, UK, Australia

ISBN: 978-93-6433-263-7 (PB)
First Published, 1918

2nd Impression 2024

Printed at: Gyan Press, Delhi.

MAHARANA SANGA THE HINDUPAT
AUTHOR: HAR BILAS SARDA

Maharana Sāngā.

Maharana Sāngā,

The Hindupat

THE LAST GREAT LEADER OF THE RAJPUT RACE.

BY

HAR BILAS SARDA, F.R.S.L.,

MEMBER OF THE ROYAL ASIATIC SOCIETY OF GREAT BRITAIN AND IRELAND; FELLOW OF THE ROYAL STATISTICAL SOCIETY OF LONDON; FELLOW OF THE STATISTICAL SOCIETY OF BOSTON, UNITED STATES, AMERICA, &C.; AND AUTHOR OF AJMER: HISTORICAL AND DESCRIPTIVE; MAHARANA KUMBHA, AND OTHER WORKS.

AJMER:

SCOTTISH MISSION INDUSTRIES COMPANY, LIMITED.

1918.

CONTENTS.

BIBLIOGRAPHY.

Colonel James Tod's *Annals and Antiquities of Rajasthan*, Volumes I and II.

W. Erskine's *Memoirs of Bābur.*

Bhavanagar Inscriptions by Peter Peterson (English and Sanskrit).

Epigraphia Indica (Sanskrit and English).

W. Erskine's *History of India*, Volumes I and II.

Major Luard's *Bibliography of Literature dealing* with the *Central India Agency, &c.*

Sir E. C. Bayley's *History of Gujarāt* (Local Muhammadan Dynasties, Gujarāt).

M. Elphinstone's *History of India.*

A. K. Forbes' *Rās Mālā.*

J. Brigg's *Tarikhi Ferishta.*

C. Mabel Duff's *Chronology of India.*

Sir H. Elliot's *History of India* (Muhammadan Period).

Stanley Lane Poole's *Bābur.*

Tabqati Akbari by Nizamuddin Ahmad (Persian).

Maharana Yash Prakash by T. Bhur Singh of Malsisar (Hindi).

Chaturkula Charitra by T. Chatur Singh of Rupāheli, Mewar (Hindi).

Mirati Sikandari (Persian).

Muntakbabul Tawarikh by Badāuni (Persian).

Rai Mal Rāsā (a Sanskrit Manuscript).

Barwa Devidan's *Geneological Record* (Hindi Manuscript).

Mehta Nanisi's *Chronicles* (Marwadi Manuscript).

R. B. P. Gauri Shanker Ojha's *History of Sirohi* (Hindi).

Kaviraj Shyamaldas' *Vir Vinod* (a most valuable History of Mewar in Hindi).

Tarikh-i-Salatin-i-Afghana (Persian).

Tarikh-i-Daudi (Persian).

Marwar Khyāt (Hindi Manuscript).

ADDITIONS AND CORRECTIONS.

Page 1.—Bābur is generally written Babar. Mr. Vincent Smith in his admirable work, "Akbar, the Great Mogul," p. 9, gives the correct spelling as Bābur.

Pages 4 and 31.—*For* Gujrat *read* Gujarāt.

Pages 50, 56, 60, 62, 65, 66, 67.—*For* Sikander *read* Sikandar.

Page 62, footnote.—*For* prefidiously *read* perfidiously.

Page 67, line 9.—*For* Bhojat *read* Bohjat.

Pages 70, 71, 93 and 144.—*For* Gagrone *read* Gagroon.

Page 78, line 5.—*For* Husein *read* Husain.

Page 96, line 3.—*For* Mewar *read* Marwar.

Page 99, line 12.—*For* Sultan Mahmud Mirza *read* Sultan Muhammad Mirza.

Pages 103, 109 and 110.—*For* Tambal *read* Tambol.

Page 109, line 15.—*For* Jehangir *read* Jahangir.

Pages 129, 137 and 145.—*For* Silhiddi *read* Silhidi.

FOREWORD.

Maharana Sanga, the *Hindupat* (Chief of the Hindus), flourished at one of the most critical periods in Indian history. Towards the end of the twelfth century A.D., the Afghans usurped supreme power in Upper India and Hindu supremacy came to an end. With the rise, however, of Mewar and the rapid expansion of the Rāthors in Western Rajputana, the Rajputs gathered strength and the Afghan power gradually declined, and the political horizon of India showed unmistakeable signs that the time was not distant when the Rajputs would recover their lost supremacy in the country. At this juncture, Sāngā appeared on the scene to lead them to their patrimony. He was at once recognised as the leader of the Hindus. His patriotism and a high sense of duty, his generosity and high-mindedness, his heroism and his position as the head of the most powerful kingdom in Hindustan marked him out as the person best fitted to hold the exalted position to which he was called by universal consent.

Sāngā was the last of the Indian sovereigns under whom all the Rajput tribes combined to repel the foreign invader. Though leaders arose in later times and heroes performed deeds of unsurpassed valour, waged great wars, and defied the might of the mightiest empire of those times, yet never again did a Rajput arise who commanded the willing homage of the entire Rajput race and led the chivalry of Rajputana, composed of all the various Rajput tribes, to contest the crown of India with the invaders from Central Asia, whose kindred had overrun the whole of Southern Europe.

The times in which Sāngā lived were no piping times of peace or of peaceful development. They were troublous times of strife and hostility, of perpetual warfare, of heroic deeds and valourous feats, and above all, of strenuous endeavours for the maintenance of national life. Noble ideals inspired men to activity, duty and achievement. High character was held in greater esteem than cleverness or high position; honour was prized above money or advancement. Weakness, cowardice, servility were despised and spurned. Courage, manliness, valour were demanded by the times and were encouraged and appreciated. Sturdy manhood was the order of the day. Men like Prithviraj, Ajjaji, Chonda, Kanh Singh and Bida Jaitmalot flourished and beautified life. A study of those times and of the men that flourished in those days will undoubtedly enrich life in the present and help us to understand and appreciate the domestic, social and political institutions and usages of the country in the past.

This volume is the second of the series of the monographs on the great men of Rajputana who have made their mark on the History of India.

H. B. SARDA.

CHAPTER I.

MAHARANA SĀNGĀ.

MAHARANA SANGRAM SINGH, popularly called Rana Sanga, was one of the greatest of the Maharanas of Mewar. It was during his reign that Mewar reached the zenith of its power and prosperity. Sanga "was the *kallas* (pinnacle) of Mewar's glory." He was the acknowledged leader of the Hindu kings and chiefs of Western India. He is styled *Hindupat*, or the "Chief of the Hindus." Bābur, the founder of the Turk power in India, says in his *Memoirs* that Rana Sāngā was the most powerful sovereign in Hindustan when he invaded it, and that "he attained his present high eminence by his own valour and sword."[1] Eighty thousand horse, 7 Rajas of the highest rank, 9 Raos and

[1] Erskine's *Memoirs of Bābur*, page 312.

104 chieftains bearing the titles of Rawal and Rawat, with 500 war elephants, followed him into the field. The princes of Marwar and Amber (Jodhpur and Jaipur) did him homage, and the Raos of Gwalior, Ajmer, Sikri, Raisen, Kalpi, Chanderi, Boondi, Gagroon, Rampura and Abu served him as tributaries or held of him in chief."[1]

Maharana Sāngā was a worthy grandson of the celebrated Maharana Kumbha. He not only fully upheld the great traditions of the royal house of Mewar, as illustrated by the work and achievements of Bappa, Jaitra Singh, Hammir and Kumbha, but added fresh lustre to them and carried them to a pinnacle of greatness and glory never associated with any Rajput family since the passing of the Chauhān family of Ajmer.

Next to the immortal Pratap, he is the most famous of the Maharanas of Chitor. In personal heroism, chivalrous character and greatness of soul, he ranks as one of the greatest kings who have ever ruled in India. His

[1] Tod's *Annals and Antiquities of Rajasthan*, Vol. I, p. 299

valour, high character and political foresight, commensurate with the necessities of the troublous times in which he was born, raised him to the highest position in Rajputana; and if he failed to drive out of India the Turk invaders from the North-west, bring the whole of Hindustan "under one umbrella," and re-establish Hindu supremacy in India, it was due not to want of ability in him, but to the deterioration of Hindu national character, to the spirit of disunion and exclusiveness then, as now, rampant in Hindu society.

CHAPTER II.

MAHARANA RAI MAL.

MAHARANA SĀNGĀ was the third son of Maharana Rai Mal, whose father, Maharana Kumbha, had humbled the pride of Malwa and Gujrat, the two greatest monarchies of the time in India, and raised Mewar to a position of great power and prosperity.

Kumbha's assassination in A.D. 1468 by his son Udai Singh, known as Uda the *Hatiaro* (parricide), gave a terrible shock to the chieftains and people of Mewar which reverberated throughout Rajputana. Though the parricide ascended the throne at Kumbhalgarh, uneasy lay his head, and he lived in constant fear of losing the throne. Not meeting with support amongst his own vassals in Mewar, he began to squander the resources of the country to purchase the support of the neighbouring chiefs. He gave Abu to the Deora chief of Sirohi to win him to his side, and bribed Rao Jodha of Marwar with the celebrated fortress of Taragarh (Ajmer) to abstain from molesting him. The deference thus shown by Uda to the Deoras and the Rāthors, however, failed to win their regard or support. Rao Jodha's son Duda, who had established himself at Merta in Baisakh of S. 1519 (A.D. 1462), took possession of the prosperous town of Sambhar, driving out the Maharana's garrison from the place. The chiefs and the people of Mewar declined to have such a blood-stained monster as their king, and he was driven from the throne[1] by the people who recalled Udai Singh's younger brother Rai Mal from Idar,[2] and by common

[1] The following couplet is current in Mewar :—

ऊदा बाप न मारजे * लिखियो लाभे राज ।
देश बसायो रायमल * सया न एको काज ॥

Uda, you should not have killed your father. Sovereignty comes if it is one's destiny. Rai Mal populated the country; you gained absolutely nothing.

[2] Rai Mal, since his banishment by his father Maharana Kumbha, had been living with his father-in-law, the Raja of Idar.

consent crowned him as Maharana of Mewar in A.D. 1473 at Chitor.

Uda, with his two sons, Suraj Mal and Sahas Mal, wandered about the country for a while, but found no support anywhere. At last he betook himself to the hereditary enemy of his family, the Khilji Sultan of Mandu, for help to regain the throne of Mewar, and went so far as to agree to give his daughter in marriage to the Sultan. Sultan Ghiyasuddin promised assistance, but the gods decreed otherwise.

Just as Udai Singh was leaving the Sultan's palace to return to his residence Indra's bolt smote him, and the parricide lay lifeless on the ground.[1] The Sultan, however, started with a large army to assist Suraj Mal and Sahas Mal to the throne of Mewar and arrived near Chitor. Rai Mal issued from the fort and attacked the Sultan, who, being utterly defeated, fled to Mandu. He felt the disgrace of the defeat

[1] Mehta Nainsi, however, says that he resided for a time at Sojat, where he married the daughter of Prince Bagha, the son of Rao Suja of Marwar and eventually went away to Bikaner, where he died.

deeply and began to prepare a large army to avenge the disaster. When his preparations were complete, he sent his generalissimo, Zafar Khan, to plunder the eastern part of Mewar.

The Rao of Begoon, Haḍa Chachikdeva, sent intelligence to the Maharana of the capture by Zafar Khan of Kotah, Bhainsror and Sheopur. The Maharana, collecting a large army and accompanied by the Rajas and governors of Aser, Raisen, Chanderi, Narwar, Boondi, Amber, Sambhar, Ajmer, Chatsoo, Lalsot, Marot, Toda and other places, started for Mandalgarh. A sanguinary battle took place, in which Zafar Khan lost almost all the notable chiefs of his army. He fled to Mandu, pursued by the Maharana, who sacked Khairabad (near Mandu). Here Sultan Ghiyasuddin sent ambassadors with peace offerings. The Maharana accepted the *nazarana* and returned to Chitor.[1]

[1] See *Rai Mal Rāsā*. Ferishta does not mention this war, probably because it was throughout disastrous to the Sultan. He says that Ghiyasuddin did not leave Mandu after his accession to the throne and that he gave himself up to luxury and ease (Vol. IV., p. 236). This, however, is not a fact. The *Rai Mal Rāsā* (unpublished) which relates these wars is the work of a contemporary writer

Maharana Sānga.

According to the Eklingji Temple in-scription of S. 1545 (A. D. 1488) Maharana Rai Mal vanquished King Kshema in the

and was written during Rai Mal's reign. Its truth is further confirmed by the Eklingji Temple inscription, dated the *Chaitra Sud* 10th, S. 1545 (A.D. 1488) (*vide* Peter Peterson's *Bhavanagar Inscriptions*, p. 117), which in Slokas 68 and 77, distinctly mentions the defeat of Ghiyasuddin near Chitor and the victories of the Maharana over him and Zafar Khan.

यंत्रायंत्रि हलाहलि प्रविचलद्दंतावलव्याकुलं वल्गद्वा-जिवरक्रमेलककुलं विस्फारवीरारवं तन्वानं तुमुलं महासिह-तिभिः श्रीचित्रकूटे गलद्गर्वं ग्यासशकेश्वरं व्यरचयत श्रीराजमल्लो नृपः ॥ ६८ ॥

King Raja Mal deprived Ghiyāsa (Ghiyasuddin), the lord of the Shakas (Mussalmans) of his pride on (near) the Chitrukūta, who fought with instruments of capturing, gave blows with ploughs, bewildered (the enemies) with his elephants, had numerous and active troops of horses and camels, had many heroes who fought with loud war-cry and who fought with terrible blows (verse 68).

मौली मंडलदुर्गमध्यधिपतिः श्रीमेदपाटावनेर्योद्धं ग्राह्यमुदार-जाफरपरीवारोरुवीरव्रजं कंठच्छेदमचिचिपच्चितितले श्रीरा-जमल्लो द्रुतं ग्यासक्षोणिपतेः यथाद्रिपतिता मानोन्नता मौलयः ॥ ७७ ॥

battle of Dadimpur[1]. He captured Kumbha Meru after defeating the enemy, the foolish

Raja Mal, the lord of the forts in the territory of Medapāta catching hold of the crests of numerous heroes of the family of Mudārajāfar (Muzaffar) beheaded them at the fort [called] Māndala (Māndalgarh.) He also threw down the crown of King Ghiyāsa (Ghiyasuddin) raised up with pride (verse 77).

Sloka 78 (*vide* footnote on p. 10) speaks of the sack of Khairabad and the cutting down of the enemy army there. Slokas 69 and 71 recite the brave deeds of the Rajput hero Gaur, who repeatedly defeated the army of the Sultan of Malwa. It further states that on one occasion when Gaur attacked the Sultan in person, he felled the crown off the Sultan's head. On the death of Gaur, Rai Mal put up his statue on a peak of Chitor, which is named aften him. The slokas are:—

कश्चिद्वीरो वीरवर्यः शकौघं युद्धेष्वस्मिन [प्रत्यहं] संजघान तस्मादेतन्नाम कामं बभार प्राकारांशश्चित्रकूटैकशृंगं ॥ ६९ ॥

In that battle, a great hero called Gaura constantly destroyed the army of the Shakas, therefore a peak of Chitrakūta, being a portion of the fort, bears this name (Gaura), verse 69.

मन्ये श्रीचित्रकूटाचलशिखरशिरोध्यासमासाद्य सद्यो यद्योधो गौरसंज्ञो सुविदितमहिमा प्रापदुच्चैर्नभस्तत् प्रध्वस्तानेकशाकम्भरकविगलद्रक्तपूरसंपर्कदोषं निःशेषीकर्तुमिच्छुर्व्रजति सुरसरिद्वारिणि स्नातुकामः ॥ ७१ ॥

[1] खर्वर्षत्संग्रामे स्वरभसमसौ दाडिमपुरे धराधीशस्तस्माद्भवदनघः शोषितसरित् । स्खलत्कूलद्दतुलो(?)पमितमरिमा खेमकुपतिः पतन् तीरे यस्यास्तटविटपिवाटे विघटितः ॥ ६४ ॥ (*Bhavanagar Ins.*, p. 121.) This town has not been identified.

Uda with his supporters.[1] "He destroyed the mountain-like Jahirala, whose roving bands were like a thorn and who was safe on account of having found refuge in thick forests."[2] "He exacted a large fine from Mālava, after tearing up the trees round Khairabad and cut to pieces numerous Yavanas, and uprooted the families of his enemies."[3]

He constructed several reservoirs of water in Mewar—Rāmatalava with blooming lotuses—Sankara and Samayasankata having abundant water.[4]

[1] श्रीकर्णादित्यवंश्यं प्रमथपतिपरीतोषसंप्राप्तदेशं पापिष्ठो नाधितिष्ठेदिति मुदितमना राजमल्लो महीन्द्रः । तादृक्षोभूतसपक्षं समरभुवि पराभूय सूढोदयाख्यं निर्धास्या(या)गेनेथमाग्राभिख्यमभिमतैरग्रहीत्कुंभमेरुं ॥ ६६ ॥ (*Bhavanagar Ins.*, p. 121).

[2] जहीरलमहीधरं धरणिरूढचजिद्विस्रमाद्दटकटककंटकिद्रुमसमाहृतैरक्षतं । विभिद्य भिदुराशिभिर्विपुलपक्षमक्षीणवीर्यदक्षिपदिवोपलं समिति राजमल्लो विभुः ॥ ७२ ॥ (*Bhavanagar Inscriptions*, p. 121).

[3] खराबादतरून् विदार्य यवनस्कंधान्विभिद्यासिभिर्निर्दंडान्मालवजाश्मलादुपहरन् भिंदंश्च वंशान्द्विषां । स्फूर्जत्संगरखड्गभ्रष्टद्विरिधरासंचारिसेनान्तरैः कीर्त्तेर्मंडलमुच्चकैर्व्यरचयत् श्रीराजमल्लो नृपः ॥ ७८ ॥ (*Bhavanagar Ins.*, p. 121).

[4] Verses 74 to 76.

श्रीरामाख्यं सरो यमरपतिरतनोद्राजमल्लदाक्षी प्रोत्फुल्लांभोजमित्थं चि(चि)त्रमदद्रमिनो वंत संम्रेरसेकम ॥ ७४ ॥ चची-

Rai Mal knew the Sāstras[1] and was a man of extensive bounties. "He allows all to stand free and happy."[2]

The Adisvara Temple inscription of S. 1587 on the Satrunjaya Hills in Kathiawar says (verse 6) that King Rai Mal was like a wrestler among kings.[3]

When the great hero Gaura, whose glory was well known, reached the sky by being placed on the top of the peak of Chitrakūta, I believe he went to bathe himself into the waters of the Surasarit (Gangā) being desirous of freeing himself from the sin committed by touching a great quantity of blood shed from numerous Shakas destroyed (wounded).

खनचक्राकरनामधेयं महासरोभूपतीराजमल्लः । तस्मानवं यज्जल-केलिक्षोभान्नमग्निश्रियात्ते गिरिजागिरीशौ ॥ ७५ ॥ श्रीराजमल्लविभुना समयासंकटमसंकटं सलिले । संबरचुंबितरंगं सेतौ तुंगं महासरो व्यरचि ॥ ७६ ॥ (*Bhavanagar Ins.*, p. 121).

1. विदितनिखिलशास्त्रो राजमल्लस्तदुच्चैर्ज्ञन विश्रद्दयति यशोभिर्बाष्पभूपान्वचार्यं ॥ ८२ ॥ (*Bhavanagar Ins.*, p. 122).

2. दानं कांचनचारु तद्वितनुते श्रीराजमल्लो विभुर्धर्मं-स्तत्र वितन्वते विहरिणस्तिष्ठंति सर्वं सुखं ॥ ९० ॥ (*Bhavanagar Ins.*, p. 122).

3. तत्पुत्रो राजमल्लोभूद्राज्ञां मल्ल इवोत्कटः (*Epigraphia Indica*, Vol. II., p. 43).

CHAPTER III.

Sāngā and His Brothers.

Rai Mal married eleven queens[1] by whom he had 14 sons[2] and two daughters. The eldest, Prithviraj, and the third,

[1] According to the records kept by the Maharana's *barwa*, Devidān, the queens were:—

Jhala Rajdhar's daughter, Ratan Kanwar.
Rāthor Bisaji's daughter, Raj Kanwar.
Rāthor Ran Singhji's daughter, Kumkum Kanwar.
Rāthor Jodha's (King of Marwar) daughter, Bir Kanwar (Sringardevi).
Rāthor Dalpat Singh's daughter, Sagatdevi.
Rāthor Rao Maldeva's (King of Marwar) daughter, Indra Kanwar.
Solanki Raja Har Rajá's grand-daughter and Raja Lal Singh's daughter, Mahtab Kanwar.
Jhala Bhan's daughter, Mahtab Kanwar.
Deora Rao Gopji's daughter, Rajkanwar.
Deora Rao Lakhaji's daughter, Champa Kanwar.
Rāthor Rao Bajraji's daughter, Anand Kanwar.

[2] The 14 sons were: Prithviraj, Jaimal, Sangram Singh, Kalyan Mal, Fattaji, Rai Singh, Bhawani Das, Kishen Das, Narain Das, Shankar Das, Devi Das, Sunder Das, Isar Das, Veni Das. The two daughters were Damodar Kanwar and Har Kanwar.

Sangram Singh or Sāngā, both by the Jhali queen Ratan Kanwar, daughter of Jhala Rajdhar, have made permanent marks on the history of Mewar. Kanwar Prithviraj was a prince whose heroic spirit, dauntless courage and irrepressible energy made him the idol of the people. His chivalrous deeds carried his fame to the farthest corner of the country. He had

> "A frame of adamant, a soul of fire
> No dangers fright him, no labours tire."

His impetuous courage, insatiable love of adventure, a perpetual thirst for action, and tireless pursuit of glory attracted kindred spirits from all parts of the country. Thousands of heroes, belonging to different clans and different places, followed Prithviraj to partake of his glory and share his dangers.

Sangram Singh (Sāngā) was equally brave, but his courage was tempered with reflection; he was as forbearing as he was brave. The second son Jaimal, though brave, lacked the energy of

Prithviraj and the high-souled generosity of Sāngā. He was conscious that with Prithviraj as his elder brother there was little chance of his obtaining the crown. The three brothers had as a companion, Suraj Mal, their uncle, who was of the same age and was equally brave. Suraj Mal was the son of Kshem Karan and grandson of Rana Mokal. Mokal had been succeeded by the celebrated Kumbha, whose son, Rai Mal, was now on the throne of Mewar. Suraj Mal was ambitious and continually chafed under the limitations which naturally circumscribe the activities of scions of a younger branch of a royal family. He began to inspire the brothers of Prithviraj with ideas of royalty, for which position every one of them considered himself qualified by descent and personal bravery. These aspirations naturally produced discord, and as Prithviraj, Jaimal and Sāngā grew up and approached manhood, their conflicting hopes, temperaments and ambitions put an end to their fraternal affection. Their dissensions not only disturbed the peace of their father, Maharana Rai Mal, and arrested the rapid development of their country, but produced a state of affairs which was very nearly fatal to the well-being of Mewar.

One day while the three brothers and Suraj Mal were discussing their future prospects, they unanimously decided to entrust their future, as did the Roman brothers, to an omen. The priestess of Charanidevi at Nahar Magra (the tiger's mount) being near by, they repaired to her abode. Prithviraj and Jaimal entered first and seated themselves on a pallet. Sāngā followed and took his seat on the panther hide belonging to the prophetess, his uncle, Suraj Mal, with one *knee* resting thereon. Scarcely had Prithviraj disclosed their errand when the sybil pointed to the panther hide as the decisive omen of sovereignty to Sanga, with a portion to the uncle. They received the decree as did the twins of Rome. Prithviraj drew his sword and would have falsified the omen had not Suraj Mal interposed himself and received the blow destined for Sāngā, while the prophetess fled from their fury. The blow, though its force was broken by the interposition of Suraj Mal, deprived Sāngā of one eye. Suraj Mal and Prithviraj were exhausted with wounds. Unwilling to attack the heir-apparent to the throne, Sāngā left the scene with five sword cuts and the loss of an eye, and made for the sanctuary of Chaturbhuja, closely followed by Jai Mal. He reached the village Sewantri, where Rathor Bida Jaitmalot,[1] who had come there from Marwar to visit the shrine of Rup Narain, established by Rana Hammir, was standing ready to return home. As he stood accoutred for the journey, his steed standing by him, he caught sight of Sāngā riding in, bathed in blood. Bida took him to his abode, but scarcely had he attended to Sāngā's wounds when Jai Mal with his followers galloped

[1] The Jaitmalot Rāthors are descendants of Jait Mal, the younger brother of the famous Mallināthji of Mallani in Mārwar.

up and demanded Sāngā to be surrendered, threatening death to Bida in case of refusal. The chivalrous Bida, like a true Rajput, refused to give up Sāngā. He sent him away to Marwar with an escort of his own followers, himself preparing to die in defence of his guest, and in the performance of his duty as a true Kshatriya. Like the celebrated Raja Hammīr of Ranthambhore, who braved the wrath of Sultan Alauddin Khilji of Delhi, and gave up his life and his kingdom rather than give up Mir Muhammad Shah, the Moghul general of the Sultan, who had taken refuge with him, the high-souled Bida and his two sons gave up their own lives to save that of Sāngā, leaving to the world an example[1] of chivalrous devotion to duty and of self-sacrifice which will continue to shed lustre on his line, now represented by the Thakur of Kelwa in Mewar.

Sāngā passed a few days with a goatherd in Marwar and was dismissed

[1] The 3 *sati* pillars in the Rupnarain temple commemorate the event.

as too stupid to tend his cattle and "precisely like our Alfred the Great, having in charge some cakes of flour, was reproached with being more desirous of eating than tending them." Leaving Marwar, he went towards Ajmer, and purchasing a horse and arms, took service with Rao Karam Chand, the Parmār chief of Srinagar, the ancient capital of the Parmārs of this part of the country, situated at a distance of about ten miles from Ajmer. Karam Chand had a following of two or three thousand Rajputs, with which he used to "run the country."

Returning one day from one of these raids, Sāngā alighted under a banian tree and spreading his saddle cloth on the ground and placing his sword under his head reposed, his steed grazing by his side. A ray of the sun penetrating the foliage fell on Sāngā's face and discovered a snake rearing its crest over the head of the exile, and a bird of omen perching itself on the crested serpent was chattering aloud. Two Rajputs, Jai Singh Bālecha and

Janna Sindhal, passing by, saw the spectacle and reported it to their leader, Karam Chand. A goatherd "versed in the language of the birds" informed Karam Chand that he was served by royalty. The Parmar questioned the attendant of Sāngā and coming to know that the heir-presumptive of Chitor was serving him, treated him with due respect and consideration, and kept him and his secret in his protection till the tragic death of Prithviraj cleared his way to the throne.

CHAPTER IV.

KANWAR PRITHVIRAJ.

WHEN the Maharana heard of the catastrophe, he forbade Prithviraj his presence, telling him to live on his bravery. With but five horse, Jessa Sindhal, Sangam, Abho, Janna and a Bhadail Rāthor, Prithviraj quitted Mewar and made for Godwar.

The dissensions in the royal family of Mewar and the weak *regime* during the four years of Uda's reign had paralysed the administration, and in consequence, the wild tribes of the west and the mountaineers of the Aravalli so little respected the Maharana's garrison of Nadole, the seat of the Godwar Government, that they carried their depredations to the plains. Prithviraj determined to subjugate the insurgents and restore order in Godwar, and show his father that he was possessed of resources independent of his birth.

The country was infested with Meenas, who issuing from their fastnesses had set up petty principalities. One of these chiefs, held his court at Nadolayi. Casting about for means to attain his object, and finding that his funds were running low, Prithviraj asked an Oswal merchant of the *Ojha* family for a loan, pledging his diamond ring with him. The Ojha at once recognized the ring as the one he had sold at Chitor to Prince Prithviraj, and coming to know of the enterprise on which Prithviraj was engaged, began actively to assist him. With his help, Prithviraj enlisted himself and his followers as adherents of the Meena Chief. On the approach of the hunter's festival, (Ahairea) the Meena's vassals, according to custom, obtained leave to celebrate the festival in their homes. Prithviraj, who had also obtained leave, rapidly retraced his steps and despatched his followers to attack the Meena in his stronghold, himself awaiting the result in ambush outside the gate of the town. In a short time the Meena Chief came galloping in full flight to the mountains for security. Prithviraj pursued, overtook and transfixed him with a lance to a kesola tree, and setting fire to the village, slew the Meenas as they sought to escape. He then attacked and reduced to submission, one after another, all the various Bālecha and Madrecha Chauhāns of Godwar, with the exception of the Madrecha stronghold of Desuri.

About this time (A.D. 1473—1483) Rao Lakha of Sirohi, with the assistance of Rao Bhan of Idar, attacked and killed Bhoj, the Solanki Chief of Lanch. Bhoj was a descendant of the Solanki kings of Anhalwara Patan. When driven from Patan his ancestors had moved further north and settled at Lanch, where Bhoj now ruled as an independent chief. Maharao Lakha of Sirohi, who had ascended the gadi of that State in A. D. 1451 (S. 1508) was an ambitious ruler, and he determined to take Lanch from the Solankis. He made five or six attempts to deprive Bhoj of his territory, but was defeated every time. Lakha then asked Rao Bhan of Idar to help him, and with his assistance attacked and killed Bhoj.

This battle is said to have taken place at the hill of Mālmagra.[1]

Bhoj's son, Rai Mal, and grandsons, Shankar Singh, Samant Singh, Sakhra and Bhan, left Lanch and went to Kumbhalgarh. Kanwar Prithviraj offered them the fief of Desuri, asking them to wrest it from its Madrecha Chauhān chief. Rai Mal's wife being a daughter of that chieftain, Rai Mal showed unwillingness to undertake the expedition. Finding, however, that Prithviraj was unwilling to help him on any other terms, Rai Mal accepted the offer. He with his sons went to his father-in-law's house and treacherously murdered Sanda and the other Madrecha Rajputs and obtained from Prithviraj a *patta* for Desuri with its 140 villages.[2] The Thakurs of Jilwada and

[1] Mehta Nainsi in his *Chronicles* says that Bhoj Dipawat had taken up his residence in the town of Las Munawad of Sirohi.

[2] The grant included Agaya, Bandrot, Dhamyagaon, Sewantri, Desuri, Dholana, each with twelve villages attached to it, as well as Ana, Karanawas, Bansda, Moonpura, Keshuli, Ganthi, Godla and Chauvadia. Mehta Nainsi gives further details of these villages.

Rūpnagar, descended from Rai Mal's sons, Shankar Singh and Samant Singh respectively, are amongst the 32 sardars (second-class nobles) of Mewar. Having restored order in Godwar, Prithviraj appointed the Ojha and one Solanki Rai Mal, to the civil and military governments of the province.

During the absence of Sāngā and the banishment of Prithviraj, Jai Mal was looked upon as the heir to the throne. The fame of the beauty of Tara Bai, daughter of Rao Surtan of Badnor, having reached Jai Mal's ears, he became desirous of obtaining her hand. Rao Surtan was of the Solanki tribe, the lineal descendant of the famed Balhara kings of Anhalwara. Thence expelled by the arms of Alauddin Khilji in the thirteenth century, they migrated to Central India, and obtained possession of Tonk-Toda and its lands on the Banās, which from remote times had been occupied (perhaps founded) by the Taks, and hence bore the name of Taksillanagar, familiarly Takitpur and Toda.

Surtan's brother, Sham Singh, on being deprived of Toda by the Afghan Lallakhan, had come to the Maharana, who conferred the fief of Badnor on him. Surtan succeeded him and was now Chief of Badnor at the foot of the Aravalli, within the bounds of Mewar. This fair "Star" (Tara) was a type of the highest Rajput womanhood. Stimulated by the reverses of her family, and by the incentives of its ancient glory, Tara Bai, scorning the habiliments and occupations of her sex, learned to guide the war-horse, and to throw with unerring aim the arrow from its back, even while at full speed. Armed with the bow and quiver, and mounted on a fiery Kathiawar, she joined the cavalcade in their unsuccessful attempts to wrest Toda from the Afghan. Jai Mal in person made proposals for her hand. "Redeem Toda," said the star of Badnor, "and my hand is thine." He assented to the terms; but having attempted to get a glimpse of the fair face before he had won her, he was slain in an encounter with her indignant father near Sādgaon, sixteen miles from Badnor, by the spear of Sānsla Ratan Singh. The Rana, when incited to revenge, replied "that he who had thus dared to insult the honour of a father and that father in distress, richly merited his fate."

Prithviraj, the brother of the deceased, was then an exile in Marwar; he had just signalized his valour and ensured his father's forgiveness, by the redemption of Godwar. The catastrophe at Badnor determined him to accept the gage thrown down to Jai Mal. Fame and the bard had carried the renown of Prithviraj far beyond the bounds of Mewar; the name alone was attractive to the fair, and when thereto he who bore it added all the chivalrous ardour of his Chauhān namesake and prototype, Tara Bai, with the sanction of her father, consented to be his, on his simple asseveration that "he would restore to them Toda or he was no true Rajput."

The anniversary of the martyrdom of the sons of Ali was the season chosen for the exploit. Prithviraj formed a select band of five hundred cavaliers, and, accompanied by his bride, the fair Tara, who insisted on partaking of his glory and his danger, he reached Toda at the moment the *tazzia* or bier containing the martyr-brothers was placed in the centre of the "chauk" or square. The prince, Tara Bai, and the faithful Senger Chief, the inseparable companion of Prithviraj, left their cavalcade and joined the procession as it passed under the balcony of the place in which the Afghan was putting on his dress preparatory to descending. Just as he had asked who the strange horsemen were that had joined the throng, the lance of Prithviraj and an arrow from the bow of his Amazon bride stretched him on the floor.[1] Before the crowd recovered from the panic, the three had reached the gate of the town, where their exit was obstructed

[1] The following old couplet extant in Rajputana sums up the popular view of the incident:—

भाग लल्ला प्रथिराज आयो
सिंह कै घांघरे स्याल आयो ।

Run away, Lalla, Prithviraj has arrived. A jackal has been born in a lion's den (it cannot stay there).

by an elephant. Tara Bai with her scimitar divided his trunk, and the animal fleeing, they joined their cavalcade, which was close at hand.

"The Afghans were encountered, and could not stand the attack. Those who did not flee were cut to pieces; and the gallant Prithviraj inducted the father of his bride into his inheritance.[1] A brother of the Afghan, in his attempt to recover it, lost his life.

"Nawab Malloo Khan, then holding Ajmer, determined to oppose the Sesodia prince in person; who, resolved upon being the assailant, advanced to Ajmer, encountered his foe in the camp at day-break, and after great slaughter entered Garh Beetli, the citadel, with the fugitives. 'By these acts,' says the chronicle, 'his fame increased in Rajwara: one thousand Rajputs, animated by the same love of glory and devotion, gathered round the *nakarras* of

[1] झड चढे प्रथिमल भाजे टोडो
लाला तणैं वर मारे लोड ।

Prithviraj arms himself against Lalla and heading an army breaks Toda.

Prithviraj. Their swords shone in the heavens, and were dreaded on the earth; but they aided the defenceless.'"[1]

Another instance of Prithviraj's high spirit, energy and enterprise is, says Colonel Tod, "recorded and confirmed by Muhammadan writers as to the result, though they are ignorant of the impulse which prompted the act. Prithviraj on one occasion found the Rana conversing familiarly with an *ahdy*" (a military officer) of the Malwa King, and feeling offended at the condescension, expressed himself with warmth. The Rana ironically replied: 'You are a mighty seizer of kings, but for me I desire to retain my land.' Prithviraj abruptly retired, collected his band, made for Neemuch, where he soon gathered five thousand horse, and reaching Depalpur, plundered it, and slew the governor. The King of Malwa on hearing of the irruption, left Mandu at the head of what troops he could collect. The Rajput prince, instead of retreating, rapidly advanced and attacked the camp while

[1] Tod's *Rajasthan*, Vol. I, p. 674.

refreshing after the march. Singling out the royal tent occupied by eunuchs and females, Prithviraj made Mahmud captive, and placing him on an express camel beside himself he warned the pursuers to follow peaceably or he would put his Majesty to death, adding that he intended him no harm, but that after having made him 'touch his father's feet,' he would restore him to liberty. Having carried him direct to Chitor and to his father's presence, he turned to him saying, 'Send for your friend the *ahdy*,' and 'ask him who this is.' The Malwa king was detained a month within the walls of Chitor, and having paid his ransom in horses, was set at liberty with every demonstration of honour. Prithviraj returned to Kumbhalgarh, his residence, and passed his life in exploits like these from the age of fourteen till death, the admiration of the country and the theme of the bard."[1]

The amazing rapidity with which Prithviraj moved from one place to another and the lightning-like speed with

[1] Tod's *Rajasthan*, Vol. I, p. 675.

which he marched and fell on his enemy earned for him the title of *Udnā Prithviraj*, the "winged Prithviraj."[1]

One of the earliest exploits of Prithviraj, which made him famous in Rajputana, was his daring raid on Girnār in the heart of Gujrat. Maharana Rai Mal's sister—Maharana Kumbha's daughter—Ramā Bai, had been married to Raja Mandlik Jādava (Yadava) of Surashtra (Girnār).[2]

[1] Mehta Nainsi says that Prithviraj attacked Toda and Jalor—two places separated by 200 miles from each other—on one and the same day, and that thenceforth he was called "Udnā Prithviraj."

[2] Mehta Nainsi in his *Chronicles* says that King Mandlik was a powerful ruler and commanded an army of twenty thousand Rajputs, and used to construct new tanks every year. He used to bathe every day with Ganges water and drink no water but that of the Ganges. The reason of his fall, according to Nainsi, was his uncontrolled passion for the wife of a Charan. Akho, son of Surtan, was a Charan attached to the principal gate of his fortress. His wife Nagdevi, was possessed of supernatural powers. Nagdevi's son had married a *Padmini*, whose son, Nagarjuna, went to Sultan Mahmud Begara and won his favour and obtained from him two mares named *Labah* and *Lakshmi*. From them, Nagarjuna had two horses, *Uchasaro* and *Amolak*, which became famous. Raja Mandlik hearing of their fame sent for them. The Charan refusing to give them up, the Raja himself went to Nagarjuna for them, but was no more successful than his men. After some time, a barber of the Raja happened to go to Nagdevi, who asked him

Owing to some disagreement between the husband and the wife, Mandlik began to illtreat his Queen. Prithviraj heard of this, and with a chosen band of his veterans started to punish King Mandlik. Traversing the long distance by rapid marches, Prithviraj surprised Mandlik in his palace. In his helplessness, he appealed to Prithviraj's clemency. Prithviraj spared his life, but as a mark of punishment cut a little piece off his right ear and returned with his aunt Ramā Bai, to

to pare the nails of her daughter-in-law, the Padmini. Struck by her surpassing beauty, he repaired to Mandlik and spoke to him about her. Mandlik resolved to go and see her. His queen, Ramā Bai, expostulated with him and tried her best to dissuade him. Mandlik persisted in his nefarious design and went to the village where Nagdevi lived. Nagdevi supplied the entire following of the Raja with provisions from a small *kotri* (cell) of hers. Surprised at this supernatural feat, the king's attendants told him that she was a goddess and nothing should be done to displease her. The king, mad with desire, did not listen to them. The *bar* tree under which he sat began to shoot jets of blood, but the king did not take the warning. He asked Nagdevi to show him the Padmini. The Devi brought her out properly decked, but her feet did not touch the ground. Mandlik thrust forward his hand to catch hold of her. She, however, assumed the form of a goddess and pronounced a curse upon him, that he would lose his fortress,

Mewar. The Maharana gave the parganah of Jāwar for maintenance to Ramā Bai, who, with her savings, built the temple of Ramaswami and the lake Ramkund at Jāwar (Yogini Pattan), the inauguration ceremony of which took place on Chaitra Sukla 7th (Sunday) S. 1554[1] (A. D. 1497). She also built the Damodar temple to Vishnu at Kumbhalgarh and a tank to the south of Kundeshwar.

become insane, throw dust on his head and become a slave of the Turks (Mussalmans.) Mandlik returned home and Padmini went to Kedar in the Himalayas, and like the Pandavas gave herself up to the eternal snows. Nagdevi repaired to Sultan Mahmud Begara and told him that she had bestowed Girnār on him. The Sultan, who had not been able to take the stronghold of Girnār owing to its great strength, asked for some sign of assurance of his success. The Devi said that on waking up the next morning he would find coloured rice in his turban. Finding the prophecy come true, the Sultan started to attack Girnār and laid siege to the fortress. Mandlik became mad and came and handed over the keys of the fort to the Sultan and embraced Islam. The fortress was not taken, however, till a thousand Rajputs who defended it bravely were all slain. This story shows that Mandlik by his misconduct displeased a Charan, with whose assistance, Mahmud Begara took Girnār, and that Ramā Bai left Girnār when she found that Mandlik was not behaving himself.

[1] Inscription on Ramkund at Jawar of Chaitra Sud 7th, S. 1554. Jawar is situated 5 miles from Tidi, in the Magra Zillah of Mewar.

Soon after Jai Mal's death, Maharana Rai Mal conferred the parganah of Bhainsror of the annual rental of Rs. 50,000 on Rawat Suraj Mal (Rana Mokal's grandson) as jagir. When the news of this grant reached Prithviraj in Godwar, he recollected the prophecy of the Charanidevi and the duel he had with Suraj Mal, and sent a letter to the Maharana protesting against the grant. The Maharana replied that he on his part had made the grant and that Prithviraj was at liberty to take it back if he could. As soon as this reply reached Prithviraj, he started to attack Bhainsror with two thousand horsemen. Putting Suraj Mal and Sarangdeva, a grandson of Rana Lakha, to flight, he took possession of the castle and turned the families of the two chieftains out of the fort.

Suraj Mal, whose vaunting ambition had persuaded him that the crown was his destiny, plunged deep into treason to obtain it. Winning over Sarangdeva to his cause, they both repaired to Sultan Nāsiruddin Khilji of Malwa. The Sultan welcomed the opportunity these internal dissensions in Mewar gave him to inflict a blow on Chitor, and thus avenge the defeats the successive Maharanas had inflicted on his ancestors. He sent a large army against Mewar. Thus aided, the two traitors assailed the southern frontier of their fatherland and rapidly possessed themselves of Sadri, Batarda and a wide tract extending from Nye to Neemuch, attempting even Chitor. With the few troops that were in the fort, the Maharana started to punish the rebels, who met the attack on the river Gambhiri. The Maharana, fighting like a common soldier, had received two and twenty wounds and was nearly falling through faintness when Prithviraj, who had heard of the invasion, with lightning speed arrived with one thousand fresh horse from Kumbhalgarh and averted a disaster. Looking out for his uncle Suraj Mal, he soon sighted him. Cutting his way up to him, he covered him with wounds. Both sides lost many brave men but neither would yield. When night fell they retired from the field and bivouacked in sight of each other.

Soon after nightfall, Prithviraj paid a visit to his uncle Suraj Mal, and the meeting between the rival uncle and the nephew is described by Colonel Tod as "unique in the details of strife, perhaps since the origin of man." Prithviraj found his uncle in a small tent reclining on a pallet, having just had the barber (surgeon) to sew up his wounds. He rose and met his nephew and heir to the throne of Mewar with the customary respect, as if nothing unusual had occurred; but the exertion caused some of the wounds to open afresh, when the following dialogue ensued :—

"PRITHVIRAJ. 'Well, uncle, how are your wounds?'

SURAJ MAL. 'Quite healed, my child, since I have the pleasure of seeing you.'

PRITHVIRAJ. 'But, uncle (*kaka*), I have not yet seen the Dewanji.[1] I first ran to see you, and I am very hungry; have you anything to eat?'"

[1] The Maharana is called Diwanji, owing to his being the chief priest of the famous temple of *Eklingji*.

Dinner was soon served, and the extraordinary pair sat down, and 'ate off the same platter *(thâli)*;' nor did Prithviraj hesitate to eat the '*pān*'[1] presented on his taking leave.

"PRITHVIRAJ. 'You and I will end our battle in the morning, uncle.'

SURAJ MAL. 'Very well, child; come early!'"

They met: but Sarangdeva bore the brunt of the conflict, receiving thirty-five wounds. During four *ghurries*, swords and lances were plied, and every tribe of Rajput lost numbers that day. At last the rebels were defeated and fled towards Sadri, and Prithviraj returned in triumph, though with seven wounds, to Chitor. Suraj Mal took up his abode at Sadri and Sarangdeva at Batarda. The Maharana did not wish to trouble them any further, but Prithviraj was relentless in his efforts to drive them out of Mewar. Many personal encounters took place between the uncle and the

[1] *Pān* has frequently been a medium for administering poison.

nephew: the latter saying he would not let him retain "as much land of Mewar as would cover a needle's point": and Suraj Mal retorting, that "he would allow his nephew to redeem only as much as would suffice for him to lie upon."

Driven from place to place, the rebels came to the wilds of Bāturro (Batarda), where they formed a stockaded retreat of the *dho* tree, which abounds in the forest; and one day while Suraj Mal and his companion Sarangdeva, were communing by the night fire on their desperate plight, their cogitations were checked by the rush and neigh of horses. Scarcely had the pretender exclaimed, "this must be my nephew!" when Prithviraj dashed his steed through the barricade and entered with his troops. All was confusion, and the sword showered its blows indiscriminately. The young prince reached his uncle and dealt him a blow which would have levelled him but for the support of Sarangdeva, who upbraided him, adding "a buffet now was more than a score of wounds in former days:" to which Suraj Ma added, "only when dealt by my nephew's hand." Suraj Mal demanded a parley; and calling on the prince to stop the combat, he continued: "If I am killed, it matters not—my children are Rajputs, they will run the country to find support; but if you are slain, what will become of Chitor? My face will be blackened and my name everlastingly reprobated.

"The sword was sheathed, and as the uncle and nephew embraced, the latter asked the former, 'What were you about uncle, when I came?'—'Only talking nonsense, child, after dinner.'—'But with me over your head, uncle, as a foe, how could you be so negligent?'—'What could I do? You had left me no resource, and I must have some place to rest my head.'"

There was a small temple near the stockade, to which in the morning Prithviraj requested his uncle to accompany him to sacrifice to the *mother* (*Kali*), but the blow of the preceding night prevented him from going. Sarangdeva was his proxy,

Suraj Mal having left for Sadri. One buffalo had fallen and a goat was about to follow when the prince turned his sword on Sarangdeva. The combat was desperate, but Prithviraj was the victor, and the head of the traitor was placed as an offering on the altar of *Time (Kali)*. The place was plundered and the town of Bāturro (Batarda) was recovered.

Having done with Sarangdeva, Prithviraj started for Sadri to despatch Suraj Mal after Sarangdeva. Suraj Mal having reached Sadri, stopped there only to fulfil his threat that "he would make over the lands to those stronger than the king." Among others he gave 12 villages of Debari, including Billano and Banslo to Brahmins and bards, and was about to abandon Mewar for ever when Prithviraj arrived. He was received in due form. Suraj Mal's wife placed poisoned food before the prince. Suraj Mal came to know of this, but not knowing which plate contained the poison, he was unable to remove it. He therefore sat down to join Prithviraj in the repast.

Instantly, his wife removed the plate containing the poison. Like a flash of lightning, the incident revealed the truth to Prithviraj. Overwhelmed by the solicitude of his uncle for his safety, he got up and said: "Uncle, now the throne of Mewar is at your service." Suraj Mal replied that the throne apart, he would not stay in Mewar even to drink water.

Passing through the wilds of Kanthal, he had an omen which recalled the Charani's prediction: "a wolf endeavouring in vain to carry off a kid defended by maternal affection." This was interpreted as strong ground for a dwelling. He halted there and subdued the native tribes of the jungles and erected on the spot where the wolf was held at bay by the goat, the stronghold [1] of Deolia. He became the lord of a thousand villages and founded the State, which under the name of Deolia Pratapgarh, is now one of the eighteen Ruling Chiefships of Rajputana.

[1] Mehta Nainsi in his *Chronicles* says that it was Suraj Mal's grandson, Bika, son of Bagh Singh, who took Deolia and severed his connection with Mewar.

Prithviraj was all this time in blissful ignorance of the whereabouts of Sāngā and whether he was alive or dead. Sāngā's marriage with the daughter of the Rao of Srinagar made known his retreat to Prithviraj, who determined to visit Rao Karam Chand with his vengeance for daring to give protection to Sāngā in defiance of his threats. The fates, however, willed otherwise, and this "Rolando of his age" was treacherously poisoned by his own brother-in-law, whose life he had spared.

As Prithviraj was preparing for his expedition against Karam Chand of Srinagar, he received a letter from his sister Ananda Bai, written in great grief, complaining of her ill-treatment by her lord, Rao Jug Mal of Sirohi, from whose tyranny she begged to be delivered and to be restored to her paternal roof. When Prithviraj read this letter, he was all afire with indignation and rage. Leaving aside for the present the projected attack on Srinagar, he instantly started for Sirohi, which he reached at midnight. Scaling the palace, he interrupted the slumbers of Jug Mal by placing his poniard at his throat. His wife, forgetting her husband's cruelty, responded to his humiliating appeal for mercy, and begged her brother to spare his life, which was granted on condition of his standing as a suppliant with his wife's shoes on his head and touching her feet, the lowest mark of degradation. He obeyed, was forgiven and embraced by Prithviraj. The next morning, Jug Mal entertained his royal brother at a public entertainment. At Prithviraj's departure, Jug Mal[1] presented him with three pills of a confection for which he was celebrated. Prithviraj ate them as he came in sight of Kumbhalgarh, but on reaching the shrine of Mamadevi, he was unable to proceed further. He sent a message to the fair Tara to come and bid him farewell, but so subtle was the poison that death overtook him ere she descended from the fortress. Her resolution was soon taken; the pyre was erected, and with the mortal remains of the chivalrous Prithviraj in

[1] P. Gauri Shanker Ojha's *History of Sirohi*, p. 205. Jug Mal reigned from A.D. 1483 to A.D. 1523.

her embrace, she ascended "the regions of the sun."

Such was the end of this hero of Mewar and the "Star" of Badnor. How the course of history would have run if Prithviraj had been spared to lead the fortunes of Mewar, and what fate the founder of the Turk (Moghal) dynasty in India would have met at the hands of Rajput chivalry, led by the reckless heroism and the impetuous energy of Prithviraj, instead of the cautious Sāngā, it is, as Colonel Tod says, futile to conjecture. One thing, however, is certain. If Bābur, after his early defeats had had Prithviraj instead of Sāngā as his opponent, the chances are overwhelming that he would have ended his days an unsuccessful adventurer, at Khanua, near Sikri, in February A.D. 1527, and the Indian soil have been once more cleared of the hordes from the North-west.

CHAPTER V.

EARLY YEARS OF SĀNGĀ'S REIGN.

THE shock of Prince Prithviraj's death shattered the constitution of Maharana Rai Mal, who grievously mourned the loss of his noble and heroic son, whose deeds were ringing throughout the country and whose fame had spread far and wide in the land. He fell ill, and, during his illness, news reached him that Sangram Singh was with Rao Karam Chand of Srinagar. A messenger was sent to Karam Chand, who presented himself with Prince Sangram Singh at Chitor. The Maharana was delighted to see his son again, and conferred on Karam Chand a suitable jagir as a reward for his services. His descendants still hold the village of Banberi and are amongst the thirty-two Sardars of Mewar.

Maharana Sāngā.

Rai Mal did not long survive the death of the heroic Prithviraj. He died in Vicrama Sambat 1566 (A.D. 1508), and Sangram Singh ascended the throne of Mewar on (Jeth Sud 5th, S. 1566)[1] 4th May A.D. 1508, in the renowned fortress of Chitor. Sangram Singh was born on Baisakh Bad 9th, S. 1539 [2] and was therefore 27 years old when he took his seat on the cushion of Bappa Rawal.[3]

When Maharana Sāngā came to the throne, Rajputana as a whole was much stronger politically than it had been since the advent of the Afghan power in India. After the Chauhāns of Ajmer, the Guihlots of Mewar rose to great power. Even in Kumbha's time (A.D. 1433-1468) the Guihlots were the only powerful Rajput Kingdom in Rajputana. The Hārās were the vassals of Mewar, and the Kachhwahas

[1] Mehta Nainsi's *Chronicles.* Mehta Nainsi says that Rai Mal had a son named Jassa, who was given to pleasure and sport, and the Sardars passed him over and placed Sangram Singh on the throne.

[2] Ibid.

[3] Bābur had been four years king of Kabul when Sāngā became Maharana.

(capital Amber, now Jaipur) were not of much political consequence. The Rāthors were only just beginning to strike root in the region round Mandawar (Mandor), the seat of the ancient Paṛihar power which, in Narhar Rao's time had been paramount in Hindustan.

When Sāngā came to the throne in A.D. 1508 A.D., both the Kachhwahas and the Rāthors had gathered strength and had not only become powerful neighbours of the Guihlots of Mewar, but had contributed largely in covering Rajputana with a race of warriors which first showed its strength in joining the Guihlots in offering a desperate resistance to the foùnding of the Turk power in India, and which later (Akbar's time) had to be wooed and won over before that power could strike root in the country. While the Kachhwahas had brought under their control the whole of Dhundhar (now Jaipur State) and had made Amber a powerful kingdom, the Rāthors had not only founded Jodhpur (S. 1515, A.D. 1458) and firmly established themselves in Pali, Sojat and other places, but had spread over and taken possession of the whole of the country of Jānglu, founded Bikaner (A.D. 1488) and Chāpar Dronapur (S. 1526, A.D. 1469). The Rāthors occupied the whole of Western Rajputana, with the Bhattis in the extreme west and south-west: the Kachhwahas were in Amber and were in possession of the country up to Mewat and the south-western borders of the Panjab, while the east was very nearly all dominated by the Guihlots of Mewār.

One of the earliest acts of Sāngā after his accession to the throne was to reward handsomely the services rendered to him by Rao Karam Chand, the Parmar Chief of Srinagar. The Maharana conferred the fief of Ajmer on him and enrolled him amongst the nobles of the first rank in Mewar.

Soon after his accession, Sāngā began to consolidate his dominions and recover what had belonged to Mewar but had been lost during the parricide's reign and not recovered by Rai Mal.

Sāngā's country was surrounded by the Mussalman kingdoms of Delhi, Malwa and Gujarāt except towards the west, where the Rāthors were rapidly rising to power. With all these three monarchies, Sāngā had to wage wars, and it is due to his military genius that Mewar came out successful in every one of them. Combinations were formed against him and he had to fight his enemies on all the three fronts at the same time, but his genius was equal to all emergencies. It has been recorded to his glory that he not only vanquished them and extended his kingdom at their expense but made them respect the frontiers established by him. He won the respect and attachment of all the Hindu kings of Upper India and raised Mewar to an eminence never reached by any Hindu kingdom since the fall of the Chauhan dynasty of Ajmer towards the end of the twelfth century. Sāngā's achievements raised him to a position in India which, in the words of Mr. Erskine, "inspired all his countrymen with hopes that a change of dynasty was about to take place; and they hailed with joy the prospect of a native

Government of India."[1] Had not a small incident occurred on the field of Khānua on 16th March A.D. 1527, the crown of India "might again have encircled the brow of a Hindu, and the banner of supremacy been transferred from Indraprastha to the battlements of Chitor."[2]

The early part of the sixteenth century witnessed the rapid decay of the Pathan power in Northern India. The Lodi dynasty had succeeded the Sayyads at Delhi. The fanatical Sikander transferred the seat of government to a more central position, Agra, in the vain hope of strengthening the failing sinews of the Pathan power in Hindustan, which was crumbling to pieces. The cruelty, distrustfulness and oppression of Sikander's son Ibrahim led to numerous revolts in his dominions, and the time was favourable for the designs of a vigorous monarch like Sāngā. "Mewar little dreaded these imperial puppets, when 'Amurath to Amurath

[1] W. Erskine's *History of India*, Vol. I., p. 469.

[2] Tod's *Rajasthan*, Vol. I., p. 300.

succeeded,' and when four kings reigned simultaneously between Delhi and Benares."[1]

The kingdom of Malwa, founded in A.D. 1401 by Dilawar Khan Ghori, was now, after only a century's existence, tottering to its fall. The cruelty and incapacity of Nāsiruddin had disgusted the nobles, and the administration had become weak and inefficient. Nāsiruddin was succeeded in 1511 A.D. [2] by his son, Mahmud II, who lacked all the qualities of a king except personal courage, and who consequently brought about the downfall of that kingdom.

The Sultanate of Gujarāt, founded in A.D. 1407 by the Hindu convert, Zafar Khan,[3] was a small principality. When separated from Delhi, the new king had but a narrow territory on the plain. On the north-west were the independent Rajas of Jalor and Sirohi from whom he occasionally levied contributions. The Raja of Idar, another Rajput prince, was in possession of the western

[1] Tod's *Rajasthan*, Vol. I., p. 299.

[2] Major Luard's *Bibliography, &c.*, p. 70.

[3] Bayley's *History of Gujarāt*, p 84.

part of the hills. The rest of the hilly and forest tract was held by the mountain tribes of Bhils and Kolis, among whom some Rajput princes, mostly connected with Mewar, had also founded petty States. The peninsula was in the hands of nine or ten Hindu tribes who had mostly come from Cutch and Sindh at different periods some centuries before. The real possessions of the kings of Gujarāt, therefore, only included the plain between the hills and the sea, and even of that the eastern part belonged to an independent Raja who resided in the hill fort of Champānēr. On the other hand, the Gujarāt territory stretched along the sea to the south-east so as to include the city of Surat and some of the country beyond it.[1] The Sultans maintained their power, as the Hindu Rajas were all disunited. Although none of the latter was strong enough to drive out the Sultan from Gujarāt, so powerful were these Rajas that the Sultan had at times to use all the resources of his kingdom to subdue even one of them. If they had com-

[1] Elphinstone's *History of India*, p. 673. (Edition of 1857 A.D.).

bined, the Sultanate would have ceased to exist.

When Sāngā came to the throne, the Sultanate of Gujarāt was at the meridian of its power and prosperity. Mahmud Shah Begara's reign was drawing to a close, and it was with his son, Muzaffar Shah II, who reigned till A.D. 1526, that Sāngā had to wage wars. It was through Idar that Sāngā came into collision with the Sultan of Gujarāt. Idar, as stated above, is a small Rāthor Rajput principality situated on the borders of Gujarāt. Its ruler, Rao Bhan, died, leaving two sons, Suraj Mal and Bhim. Suraj Mal succeeded to the throne but died after a reign of 18 months, leaving a minor son Rai Mal, who became Rao of Idar. He was, however, deposed by Bhim,[1] who usurped the throne. Rai Mal fled to Chitor for shelter. Bhim dying a few days after this, his son Bhar Mal, became Rao of Idar. Rai Mal on growing up to manhood claimed his patrimony, and with the assistance of Maharana

[1] A. K. Forbes' *Ras Mala*, p. 290 (1878 edition).

Sāngā,[1] about A.D. 1514, regained Idar, expelling Bhar Mal, who appealed for help to Sultan Muzaffar[2] of Gujarāt. The Sultan at the time was on the borders of Malwa watching developments in that country. When the envoys of Bhar Mal reached Muzaffar, he sent Nizam-ul-mulk with an army to reinstate Bhar Mal on the *gadi* of Idar. The *Mirat-i-sikandari* says that "in A.D. 1517, Rai Mal fought with the Gujarāt armies and was sometimes defeated and sometimes victorious."[3] Ferishta says that Rai Mal was defeated and that he retired to the hilly tract of Bijanagar.[4] Nizam-ul-mulk after reinstating Bhar Mal on the *gadi* of Idar, went in pursuit of Rai Mal. Rai Mal issued from the hills and attacked the Gujarāt army. In the battle that took place, Nizam-ul-mulk was severely defeated[5] and his best officers and soldiers

[1] Bayley's *Gujarāt*, p. 252. Brigg's Ferishta, Vol. IV., p. 83.

[2] Brigg's Ferishta, Vol. IV., p. 83. *Ras Mala*, p. 293.

[3] Bayley's *Gujarāt*, p. 253.

[4] Ferishta, Vol. IV., p. 83.

[5] Ferishta, Vol. IV., p. 83 ; also *Ras Mala*, p. 294.

were slain. The Sultan thereupon recalled Nizam-ul-mulk to Ahmadabad.

In A.D. 1517, Rai Mal, assisted by the Maharana[1] re-entered the Idar territory. The Sultan of Gujarāt sent his general Zahir-ul-mulk, with a large army against him. Zahir-ul-mulk was, however, attacked by Rai Mal and defeated with great slaughter.[2] Zahir-ul-mulk was killed at the head of his cavalry and the Sultan's army fled to Gujarāt. The Sultan now sent Nasrat-ul-mulk, but he too failed to achieve any success against Rai Mal, who continued to ravage the country.

---

[1] K. Shyamaldas' *Vir Vinod* and Briggs' Ferishta, p. 83.

[2] A. K. Forbes' *Ras Mala*, p. 294.

CHAPTER VI.

WAR WITH SULTAN IBRAHIM LODI.

ON the death of Sultan Sikander Lodi in A.D. 1517, his son Ibrahim succeeded him. He was engaged in putting down the revolts of his nobles, when news of Sāngā's encroachments reached him. He prepared an army and marched against Mewar. The Maharana advanced to meet him and the two armies met near the village of Khatoli on the borders of Haravati (Haraoti). The Delhi army could not stand the onslaught of the Rajputs, and after a fight lasting two *pahars* (5 hours), it gave way and fled, followed by the Sultan himself, leaving a Lodi prince prisoner in the hands of Sāngā. The prince was released after a few days on payment of a ransom.[1] In this battle, the Maharana lost his left arm by a sword cut, and an arrow made him lame for life.

[1] Duff's *Chronology of India*, p. 271.

An incident which occurred about this time illustrates the Hindu ideal of kingship. That ideal was not that of dominating the will of the people, and of ruling the country as of inalienable personal right. The ideal was that the king was the chief executive officer of the people, that he was to subordinate personal comfort, ambition and activity to their general welfare, to look upon administration as a duty rather than a right, and to resign the position as soon as the qualification necessary for rendering service was lost.

It was after long treatment that the Maharana's wounds received in the battle against Ibrahim were healed and the Maharana restored to health. In order to celebrate the occasion, the Maharana invited the friendly kings to a Darbar, where the entire vassalage and nobility of Mewar assembled to do homage to their sovereign, and tender their congratulations to him on his recovery. When the nobles and the chieftains of Mewar and the chiefs and kings of neighbouring States had assembled, the Maharana entered the grand assembly in due form. He was duly greeted on his entry into the Darbar. But contrary to the usual practice of raising both hands only up to the chest, as is the established custom of the kings of Mewar, the Maharana raised his right hand up to the head and bowed to those present. The whole assembly was filled with astonishment, which was increased when, on the nobles taking their accustomed seats, the Maharana instead of occupying the royal throne, took his seat on the floor, like other nobles. Whispers filled the hall, some going so far as to suggest that long illness had affected the mind of the Maharana. At last Rawat Ratan Singh of Salumbar, with due respect, enquired of the Maharana the reason of his returning their greetings in an unusual manner and of taking his seat below the throne, and thus acting against the established usages of the crown. On this, the Maharana got up, and raising his voice so as to make it audible to those sitting in the furthest corners of the hall declared that it was an ancient and well-established rule in India that when an idol was injured and a part of it knocked off, it ceased to be a fit object of worship, and another one was installed in its place. Similarly, the royal throne being a place of worship for the people, its occupant should also be a person who is entire and who is able to render full service to the State; that he had lost one arm and the full use of a leg, in addition to an eye, and was therefore, in his own opinion, no longer fit to occupy the throne to which all did homage. He consequently requested the whole assembly to elect as their sovereign one whom they considered a fit person to fill that exalted position, and to bestow upon him (Sāngā) suitable maintenance, so that he might continue, like other *sāmants* (warrior nobles) to serve the State for the rest of his life.

On hearing this, the assembled kings and chiefs submitted that the heroic Maharana had received injuries on a field of battle, where he had, by heroism and valour, defeated the enemy and won victory for Mewar, and that he had, therefore, not lost anything, but had become adorned with laurels, and was, in consequence, the fittest person to enhance the glory of that exalted throne. Thereupon Raja Viramdeva of Merta and other chiefs got up, and taking Sāngā by the hand placed him on the unoccupied throne.

The resources of Ibrahim were so crippled by this war with Sāngā that he could not renew the contest for some time. However, he carefully nursed his desire to be revenged on Maharana Sāngā for the disastrous defeat inflicted by the latter at Khatoli. And when the rebellion of Islam Khan, which had assumed serious proportions, was suppressed, the Sultan began to prepare an army to attack Mewar. The foremost generals of the kingdom, Mian Husain Khan Zar Bakhsh, Mian Khan Khānān Farmuli and Mian Māruf "who were the chief commanders in the army of Sultan Sikander" and "were the bravest men of the age and could have instructed even Rustam in the art of war"[1] led this expedition, with Mian Makhan as

[1] Elliot's *History of India*, Vol. V., p. 16.

commander-in-chief. When this army reached the Maharana's territory the Maharana advanced with his Rajputs. As the two armies came in sight of each other near Dholpur,[1] Mian Makhan made dispositions for the battle. Said Khan Furat and Haji Khan with 7,000 horsemen, were placed on the right; and Daulat Khan, Allahdad Khan and Yusuf Khan commanded the centre. The Sultan's army was fully prepared to give the Maharana a warm reception. The Rajputs, with their accustomed valour, advanced and fell on the Sultan's army, and in a short time put the enemy to flight. "Many brave and worthy men were made martyrs and the others were scattered."[2] This battle took place about A.D. 1518.

The Rajputs pursued the fleeing remnants of the Sultan's army up to Byana.[3]

[1] Erskine's *History of India*, Vol. I., p. 480.

[2] *Tarikhi Salatini Afghana* in Elliot's *History of India*, Vol. V., p. 19.

[3] *Tarikhi Daudi*. The *Tarikhi Salatini Afghana* says that before the battle, Mian Husein Khan separated from the Sultan's army with a thousand horsemen and joined the Rana, but that he himself did not take part in the battle, though

By this victory all that part of Malwa which had been usurped by Muhammad Shah (Sahib Khan), younger brother of Sultan Mahmud Khilji II of Mandu, during his rebellion against his brother, and had subsequently been taken possession of by Sultan Sikander Lodi, father of Sultan Ibrahim, now fell into the hands of the Maharana. Chanderi was one of the many places which fell into the hands of the Maharana,[1] who bestowed it on Medni Rai.

---

his elephants were visible, and that after the battle he sent a message reproaching Mian Maruf, saying: "It is a hundred pities that 30,000 horsemen should have been defeated by so few Hindus" (Elliot's History of India, Vol. V, page 19). It further states that while the Maharana's army was rejoicing and amusing itself after the victory, Mian Husein, now joined by Mian Maruf, prefidiously fell upon it and routed it. The *Tarikhi Daudi* and *Wakiat Mushtaki*, however, make no mention of this treacherous attack, which in view of the fact that these men had only a small following of their own, can hardly be believed to have taken place. The fact that the Maharana obtained as a result of the war a large part of Malwa and tracts up to Byana, belies this second attack. And the fact that Sultan Ibrahim Lodi had Mian Husein assassinated shortly after at Chanderi and gave rewards to the assassins, further negatives the attack.

[1] Erskine's *History of India*, Vol. I, page 480.

CHAPTER VII.

Capture of Malwa and Sultan Mahmud Khilji II.

In Malwa, developments were taking place which soon brought about the downfall of the Pathan monarchy of that country. Though Sultan Mahmud Khilji II was on the throne, the real power was in the hands of a clique of Mussalman nobles who wished to keep Mahmud a puppet in their hands. Their domineering[1] conduct towards the king made him fear for his life, and when they began openly to defy him, he fled from Mandu. This was the signal for an open revolt. The nobles headed by Mahafiz Khan, placed the crown on the head of his brother prince, Sahib Khan, and proclaimed him Sultan of Malwa. Raja Medni Rai, a powerful Rajput chieftain of Malwa, came to the Sultan's

[1] Brigg's Ferishta, Vol. IV, p. 246.

assistance. He was followed by others. The king owed his life and his throne to the fidelity and chivalry of Medni Rai, who now became the Sultan's commander-in-chief. When Sultan Mahmud marched towards the capital, he was opposed by the rebel forces, headed by Prince Sahib Khan. "The fate of the action," says Ferishta, "was eventually decided[1] by the gallant conduct of Medni Rai and the Rajput infantry, who preserved a compact phalanx, and with spears and daggers broke the enemy." Medni Rai is said to have raised a force of forty thousand Rajputs[2] to help the Sultan. The Sultan regained his kingdom with the assistance of Medni Rai, who now became Prime Minister of Malwa. He not only reduced the rebel nobles to submission but established the authority of the king throughout the kingdom. Some of these disaffected persons, jealous of his increasing power and prestige, and resenting the

[1] Brigg's Ferishta, Vol. IV, page 248.

[2] Bayley's *Gujarāt*, page 247, footnote.

restraint, the subordinate position to which they had now been reduced, imposed on them, began to intrigue against Medni Rai, and appealed to Sultan Sikander Lodi of Delhi and Sultan Muzaffar Shah II of Gujarāt for help, representing to them that Malwa had been dominated by the Hindus, and that the Sultan was such only in name. Bohjat Khan, the governor of Chanderi, revolted and invited Sahib Khan, the rebel brother of Sultan Mahmud II, to Chanderi to head the rebellion. On reaching Chanderi, Sahib Khan was met by Bohjat Khan and Mansur Khan, another rebel noble of Malwa, and was crowned King of Malwa, under the title of Sultan Muhammad, Bohjat Khan becoming his minister. In response to the rebels' appeal, Sultan Sikander Lodi sent a force of 12,000 cavalry,[1] under the command of Imadul Mulk and Sayeed Khan, to help Sahib Khan to the throne of Malwa. Sultan Muzaffar Shah of Gujarāt also started to help the rebels.

[1] Brigg's Ferishta, Vol. IV, page 253.

Sikander Khan, governor of Bhilsa, joined the rebellion[1] and began to plunder the country.

With consummate ability, Raja Medni Rai overcame all opposition, vanquished the combination of the Sultans of Gujarāt and Delhi and extricated Malwa from the difficulties that thus surrounded it. Directing Malik Lado to oppose Sikander of Bhilsa, Medni Rai marched, accompanied by Sultan Mahmud, against the forces of Gujarāt, which had arrived not very far from Mandu. Muzaffar Shah was attacked and defeated with great slaughter, and fled to Ahmadabad.[2] The Sultan of Gujarāt being thus disposed of, Medni Rai advanced to attack the Chanderi confederates. His diplomacy no less than his generalship eventually defeated the designs of the rebels. "Hearing of the advance of the Malwa troops, Sultan Sikander Lodi, unable to spare more troops at the time,

[1] Brigg's Ferishta, Vol IV, page 254.

[2] Brigg's Ferishta, Vol. IV, page 254.

ordered his contingent to fall back on Delhi. Prince Sahib Khan's forces, under Muhafiz Khan and Khwaja Jahan, marched by a circuitous route to invest Mandu. Medni Rai sent a large force of Rajputs to oppose it. A battle took place near Nalchā, in which Muhafiz Khan was killed and the rebels were completely defeated."[1] Bhojat Khan and Sahib Khan now sued for peace, which was granted. Raisen, Bhilsa and Dhamoni were given to Sahib Khan for maintenance. To relieve his immediate wants, a sum of ten lakhs of tunkas[2] was sent to the prince, which, however, was embezzled by Bohjat Khan. This occasioned an open quarrel between the prince and his minister, and Bohjat Khan was forced to flee to the Delhi Court. Prince Sahib Khan dying soon after, his minor son was taken away to Delhi by Sultan Sikander Lodi, who sent his officers to take up the adminis-

[1] Brigg's Ferishta, Vol. IV, page 256.

[2] Brigg's Ferishta, Vol. IV, page 256. The *Muntakkhabul Tawarikh* says that 11 lakhs were sent.

tration of the province of Chanderi[1] under the Delhi Government. Medni Rai thus vanquished the enemies of Sultan Mahmud Khilji and secured for him undisputed supremacy in Malwa.[2]

The disappointed and defeated nobles now began to sow distrust in the mind of Sultan Mahmud himself and to poison his mind against Medni Rai. They succeeded so far as to persuade that weak and incapable ruler to embark on the assassination of his benefactor and chief support to his throne. The Sultan made the attempt but failed to achieve his object. Medni Rai escaped wounded to his residence. The army called upon Medni Rai to depose the king, but Medni Rai not only forgave Sultan Mahmud

[1] Erskine's *History of India*, Vol. I, page 480.

[2] Mr. Erskine says: "Medni Rai was a very distinguished personage in his time. He had been the means of placing and confirming the reigning king, Sultan Mahmud Khilji, on the throne of Mandu; and supported by his Rajputs, had defeated various pretenders to the crown, in bloody battles."—*History of India*, Vol. I, page 480.

but offered to continue to serve him.[1] The weak Sultan, however, left Mandu[2] and fled towards Gujarāt. With the help of a Rajput named Kishna, he reached the village of Bhakorah, on the frontiers of Gujarāt, where the Gujarāt governor of Dohud received him hospitably and reported the matter to Sultan Muzaffar Shah at Ahmadabad. The latter sent Mahmud "the white canopy and the scarlet pavilion," signs of royalty, and a considerable body of troops. In a few days, Sultan Muzaffar himself followed with his army to reinstate Mahmud on his throne. Medni Rai expressed his sorrow at the folly of Mahmud in thus compromising the honour[3] of Malwa,

[1] Brigg's Ferishta, Vol., IV, page 259.

[2] Ibid, page 259. Ferishta calls the Sultan "a fool in the cabinet."

[3] The *Mirati Sikandari* says that though Mahmud fled, Medni Rai made no difference whatever in the expenses of Mahmud's harem. Provisions and clothes, perfumes and money were supplied as before, and eunuchs attended to it as usual. Medni Rai declared in open Durbar that he had done nothing disloyal, and that they should write to the Sultan to return and assume care of the country and appoint another Vazier.—Bayley's *Gujarāt*, pp. 262-263.

but finding that Mahmud was incorrigible, he left a garrison in Mandu for the defence of the fort and himself went to Chitor to appeal to the Maharana for aid. The Maharana only promised to march to his frontiers and await developments and to see that no harm was done to Medni Rai. He reached Sarangpur, but hearing that Mandu had fallen and that Mahmud had again assumed government he returned with Medni Rai to Chitor, as there was nothing further to be done. He, however, bestowed on Medni Rai the pargannahs of Gagrone, Chanderi and some others. Medni Rai's son, Bhimraj,[1] took up his residence at Gagrone. Sultan Muzaffar Shah also returned to Gujarāt, leaving a strong force under Asaf Khan in Malwa to support Mahmud Khilji.

Sultan Mahmud was a prince not only weak and incapable but devoid of

[1] Mehta Nainsi in his *Chronicles*, says that Maharana Sāngā had conquered Chanderi from Baghela Mukand of Bardhwa.

common sense, political foresight and judgment. Encouraged by the presence of troops left for his protection by the Sultan of Gujarāt, he determined to invade the territory of Medni Rai, and in S. 1575 (H. 925 = A. D. 1519) marched against Gagrone. As Medni Rai held this district along with others as a fief from Maharana Sāngā, the latter resolved to punish Sultan Mahmud for this temerity: for, while the latter's conduct towards Medui Rai gave evidence of his ungratefulness and want of sense, this attack on Gagrone showed that he was incapable of appreciating the forbearance and restraint of the Maharana, and was quite unmindful of the rights of peaceful neighbours. Maharana Sāngā advanced with a large army from Chitor reinforced by the Rathors of Merta under Rao Viramdeva, and met Sultan Mahmud Khilji, accompanied by the Gujarāt auxiliaries under Asaf Khan. The Sultan's forces fought bravely but could not withstand the furious onslaught of the Rajputs and sustained a complete defeat. Most of his officers were killed and the army was nearly annihilated. Asaf Khan's son was killed, and Asaf Khan himself sought safety in flight. Sultan Mahmud was taken prisoner, wounded and bleeding. The noble Maharana had him removed with care to his own camp, where his wounds were carefully dressed and properly treated. He was then removed to Chitor, where he remained a prisoner for three months. Every comfort was provided for him, and when his wounds were healed up and he was restored to health, the high-souled Maharana, with a magnanimity unique in the annals of warfare, not only set him free[1] but restored his dominions to him, and sent him to Mandu with a strong Rajput escort.

The Maharana used to treat Sultan Mahmud with great courtesy and friendship, so far at times as to make him sit on a

[1] A poet says :—

भाखां पकड़ छोड़बो सांगा थारे खांसा खेल हमीरहरा.

"Sāngā, descendant of Hammir, to capture and set free kings is a joke and play for thee.

portion of his own *gaddi* in the Darbār. One day while the Sultan was so seated, some flowers were brought up, and the Maharana taking up, a *turra* (bunch) was about to give it to the Sultan, when the latter said that there were two ways of giving a thing, either to hold your hand up and bestow it on an inferior or to keep your hand low and tender it to a superior. The latter course, continued the Sultan, was out of the question, he being the Maharana's prisoner. Nevertheless the Maharana might remember that it was not for him (Sultan) to extend his palm like a suppliant *merely* for a bunch of flowers. The Chief of the Hindus was pleased to hear this from the Sultan and generously said that half the kingdom of Malwa went with the bunch of flowers.[1] The Sultan was filled with joy at this condescension of the Maharana, and gladly extended his palm and took the flowers. The third day the Maharana bade farewell to the Sultan and sent him with an escort to Mandu and seated him on

[1] Mehta Nainsi's *Chronicles*.

the throne. As a mark of subjection, the Sultan yielded to the Maharana as *nazrana* the jewelled crown and belt left as a family heirloom by Sultan Hoshang, the first king of Malwa. The Maharana also kept at Chitor a son of the Sultan as hostage for his future good conduct.

It is difficult to characterise this clemency of the Maharana as a piece of sound policy. Though the historian Abul Fazal gives unstinted praise to the Maharana, and Nizam-ud-din Ahmad, the bigoted author of *Tabqati Akbari*, extols this act as an act of unprecedented munificence and magnanimity, yet, judged by its political results, the act has proved injurious to the national cause of the Rajputs. A true Rajput, however, is ordinarily incapable of taking a coldly political view of things. He is a hero, not a politician. Chivalry is his profession. His ideal is "to die well in battle," not "to win it." The one aim of a true Rajput is "to make his mother's milk resplendent," to perform deeds of valour and "die a glorious death," not to win a battle by skill, strategy or scheming. A true *kṣhtriya* (Hindu warrior) never hits below the belt or behind the back, and he warns the enemy before he attacks him. The ideals that nurture his soul are spiritual, not material; not "of the earth, earthy"; they are higher, nobler than those which animate other races or nations. They produce men of sublime character but not successful men of business. "To spare a prostrate foe is the creed of the Hindu cavalier," says Colonel Tod, "and he carries all such maxims to excess." He recks not of the grave consequences which follow an act of political indiscretion. He displays whenever occasion occurs, generosity, magnanimity and charity to match his heroism in war, exhibiting an utter disregard of self, hoping thereby to leave an example of a life nobly ended, to be admired by posterity.

Generosity towards a foe whose enmity is implacable, whose hatred is unquenchable, whose ideals are low, whose one aim is to destroy all who oppose him, to whom destruction of an alien is enjoined by his faith, is an act of folly, suicidal in its effect, and fatal to the cause of the nation. But the latter-day Hindu judges an act not by its consequences but only by its theoretical character. This fatal defect in the character of the Hindus led to their political subjection to people of much inferior moral calibre and much lower civilization, such as those that came from the north-west. This feature of his character finds illustration throughout history. If the cruel Hun invader, Mihirgula, had not been set free and sent home after his defeat and capture by King Bālāditya of Magadha, about 528 A. D.; if Shahbuddin Ghori, (Muhammad Bin Sām) had not been liberated after his defeat and capture by the chivalrous emperor Prithviraj, in the nineties of the twelfth century; if Mahmud Khilji I of Mandu had not been set free by Maharana Kumbha, about 1440 A. D.; if Mahmud Khilji II had not been liberated and escorted back to the throne of Mandu after his defeat and capture, in A. D. 1519; if the chivalrous Maharana Raj Singh had not spared Aurangzeb when he was completely surrounded by the Rajputs; and if Aurangzeb's son, Prince Muazzam, had not been permitted to depart unmolested when at the absolute mercy of the heir of Mewar (Jai Singh) during Aurangzeb's thirty years' war with the Rajputs, the history of India would in all probability have taken a different course. "But for repeated instances of an ill-judged humanity," says Colonel Tod, "the throne of the Moghuls might have been completely overturned." [1]

---

[1] *Annals and Antiquities of Rajasthan*, Vol. I, page 379.

CHAPTER VIII.

Invasion and Conquest of Gujarāt.

Owing to his failure to cope with Rai Mal, Nasrat-ul-mulk was removed from the government of Idar by Sultan Muzaffar Shah, who appointed "in his place, Malik Husein Bahmani, entitled Nizam-ul-mulk, a man renowned for bravery."[1]

It is said that one day (1520 A. D.) a *Bhat* (minstrel) extolled the bravery and generosity of Maharana Sāngā in open Durbar in Nizam-ul-mulk's presence and said: "He protects Rai Mal, the Raja of Idar, and though you may stay a little while in Idar, it will eventually come back into the hands of Rai Mal." This slap on the face of the governor by a common minstrel roused his anger and he exclaimed, "How can Sāngā protect Rai

[1] Bayley's *Gujarāt*, p. 264.

Mal?" adding, "Here I sit: why does he not come?" The bard replied that he was coming soon, on which Nizam-ul-mulk used disrespectful language towards the Maharana.

When this incident came to the knowledge of the Maharana he decided to invade Gujarāt and punish the impertinent governor of Idar. Sultan Muzaffar Shah of Gujarāt on being apprised of the Maharana's invasion, sent reinforcements under Asad-ul-mulk, Ghazi Khan, Shuja-ul-mulk and Saif Khan, to Nizam-ul-mulk. He appointed Qiwam-ul-mulk, governor of his capital Ahmadabad, to bear the brunt, and himself retired to Muhammadabad instead of advancing to meet the Maharana.

The Maharana started with 40,000 horse and infantry and soon arrived at Vāgadh, where Rawal Udai Singh of Dungarpur joined him with his forces. Rao Ganga of Jodhpur with 7,000 men, and Rao Viramdeva of Merta with 5,000 Rajputs, also joined the Maharana here.[2] From Vāgadh

[2] *Chaturkula Charitra*, p. 25. Rao Viramdeva had married Rana Rai Mal's daughter—Sanga's sister.

the Maharana came down swiftly upon Idar. Nizam-ul-mulk (now entitled Mubariz-ul-mulk) was alarmed at the news of Sāngā's advance towards Idar, and forgetting his vaunt, fled to the safe refuge of the fort of Ahmadnagar. The Maharana arrived at Idar the day following Mubariz-ul-mulk's flight. After reinstating Rai Mal on the throne of Idar,[1] thus restoring his patrimony to him, the Maharana started in pursuit of Mubariz-ul-mulk and laid siege to Ahmadnagar. Dunger Singh Chauhan, a notable Rajput officer of the Maharana's army[2] was seriously wounded in the assault.

[1] The Maharana demolished the great mosque at Idar and built a temple in its place.

मेलैदल सबलकसाधर मोकल ।
नांम सहें सुरताणा नाद ॥
ईडर थकी मजीत ऊथापे ।
थै ईडर थपया प्रसाद ॥

(O! powerful Rana Sāngā, following the example of Mokal, thou subjugateth Sultans and listeneth to their humble voice. Thou hast demolished the mosque of Idar and built in its place a temple).

[2] Mehta Nainsi says that Dungersi was a great Rajput, and had remained in Vagadh (Dungarpur) for some time and that Maharana Sāngā conferred Badnor on him. He adds that his sons and nephews all lost their lives in the siege of Ahmadnagar.

His son, Kanh Singh, by an act of heroism and self-sacrifice, paralleled only by the achievement of Balloo Saktawat during Maharana Amar Singh's attack on the fort of Ontala, then held by the Imperial garrison in Emperor Jahangir's reign, earned undying glory as a Rajput hero. When the moment for storming the fort came, the elephants refused to force open the gates, owing to the long iron spikes upon them. In that emergency, Kanh Singh rushed to the gate, covered the spikes with his body and urged the elephant to force the gates open, himself being impaled on the spikes. This act of heroism sent a thrill of enthusiasm through the Maharana's army, while it struck terror into the hearts of the Sultan's garrison inside the fort. The Rajputs rushed into the fort, sword in hand, and slaughtered the garrison, Mubariz-ul-mulk again fleeing by the back door of the fort. Just as he was making his exit from the fort, the same bard as had told him in open Darbār at Idar that Sanga would soon come and drive him out of Idar, appeared and taunted him on his flight, and put him to shame for continually showing the white feather before the Maharana. This stung Mubariz-ul-mulk to the quick, and he halted on the further bank of the river that flows by the fort and drew up his troops, which had been reinforced by the army sent by the Sultan from Ahmadabad, to oppose the Maharana's advance. As soon as the Maharana came to know of it, he fell upon this army and put it to flight.[1] Mubariz-ul-mulk fled towards Ahmadabad, but fearing pursuit, he left the direct road and took a circuitous route. Asad-ul-mulk and others feeling the disgrace involved in taking such a course kept on to the ordinary route, but they were pursued and slain to the last man, their elephants and equipage falling into the hands of the

[1] A. K. Forbes' *Rasmala* says: "The array of Islam was broken by the fury of Rajputs, several officers of distinction were killed; Mubariz-ul-mulk himself was severely wounded; his elephants were taken, and the whole force was driven in confusion towards Ahmadabad. Sāngā Rana now plundered the surrounding country at his leisure: he spared the Brahmans of Wadnagar, but finding Visalnagar defended against him, he took it by assault, slaying the Muhammadan governor. Having thus revenged himself for the insult which had been offered to him, he returned, unopposed, to Chitor."—p. 295.

Maharana's commanders. The Maharana took the town of Ahmadnagar and sacked[1] it and carried away captive the Mussalman inhabitants. He marched the next day to plunder Vadnagar. Arriving there, he found the town inhabited by Brahmans, who prayed for protection. Their prayers were granted and the town was left unmolested. The Maharana advanced to Visalnagar, killed the governor Hatim Khan[2] in an action that followed, and plundered the town. After plundering Gujarāt a little longer and finding that the Sultan dared not come to the protection of his subjects, and thinking that the braggart Nizam-ul-mulk (Mubariz-ul-mulk) had been sufficiently punished and taught a good lesson, and seeing that the Rao of Idar had been restored to his patrimony, the Maharana returned in triumph to Chitor.

---

[1] Bayley's *Gujarāt*, p. 269.

[2] Ibid.

CHAPTER IX.

Failure of Sultan Muzaffar Shah's Invasion of Mewar.

The Sultan of Gujarāt left Muhammadabad and returned to his capital after the Maharana had returned to Mewar. He was grieved to see his country devastated, and began to think of avenging its ruin. He set about preparing a large army, doubled the pay of the soldiers, and gave them a year's salary in advance. At last in Muharrum H. 927 (*Pos Sud* S. 1577), December A.D. 1520, the Sultan sent Malik Ayaz with an army of 100,000 cavalry, 100 elephants and a large park of artillery[1] against Mewar. Another army, consisting of 20,000 horse and 20 elephants was sent under Qiwam-ul-mulk to co-operate with Malik Ayaz. Both these armies marched to Morassa. While

[1] Bayley's *Gujarāt*, p. 271.

they were encamped there, the Sultan, according to the *Tabqati Akbari*, sent reinforcements under Taj Khan and Nizam-ul-mulk. The Sultan's army ravaged Dungarpur and advanced towards Banswara. After a skirmish between 200 horsemen under Shuja-ul-mulk and others, and some Rajputs in the hills, the Sultan's army advanced and invested the fort of Mandsaur in Malwa, then in the Maharana's possession. The governor of the fort, Asoka Mal, was killed but the fort did not fall. The Maharana left Chitor with a large army and arrived at the village of Nandsa, 12 *cos* (24 miles) from Mandsaur. In the mean-time, Sultan Mahmud Khilji of Malwa arived from Mandu to assist the Gujarāt forces to repay the debt he owed to Muzaffar Shah.

The siege was pressed but no progress was made. The Maharana was reinforced by Medni Rai's army, and Raja Silhidi, the Tuar Chief of Raisen, joined the Maharana with ten thousand cavalry. The *Mirati Sikundari* says that "all the Rajas of the country round, went to the support of the Rana. Thus on both sides enormous forces were assembled. But the enterprise of Malik Ayaz did not advance in consequence of the ill-feeling entertained against him by the Amirs...... .....No progress was made in the siege of the fort." It is probable that Sultan Mahmud Khilji, who had personal experience of the irresistible charge of the Rajput cavalry warned the Gujarāt generals of the impending disaster to their arms, and advised them to make peace and return home. Malik Ayaz foreseeing the ruin of his forces in the prolongation of the struggle made peace and fell back on Khiljipur,[1] and eventually retreated to Gujarāt.

[1] The Persian historians attribute the opening of peace negotiations by Malik Ayaz to ill-feeling between him and Qiwam-ul-mulk, the additional convenient reason as usual being that the Maharana offered his submission. The *Mirati Sikandari* says that Malik Ayaz was commander-in-chief and was in command of the main army consisting of 100,000 cavalry and artillery, and that Qiwam-ul-mulk had only 20,000 men under him, and that the latter and Sultan Mahmud Khilji were anxious to fight. Further on it says that Mahmud Khilji dissuaded Qiwam-ul-mulk from going against the wishes of Malik Ayaz, who

The Sultan is said to have received Malik Ayaz coldly when the latter waited on him at Chapaneri. The *Mirati Sikandari* says that not only was the Sultan very cold to Ayaz, but that all the people of Gujarāt called him a coward.[1]

Rao Bhar Mal of Idar who had succeeded Rai Mal outlived Muzaffar II as well as his sons Sikandar and Mahmud II, and was alive in A.D. 1530 when Bahadur Shah of Gujarāt

wished to make peace. It is thus quite clear that there was nothing whatever to prevent Malik Ayaz from continuing the war. He, however, saw the hopelessness of gaining a victory, and foresaw how disastrous would be his retreat to Gujarāt with the valiant Rajputs pursuing him in a country infested with enemies.

[1] Bayley's *Gujarāt*, page 275. This coldness was natural after the signal failure of the Malik in the expedition, which had been entrusted to him at his own entreaty. The statement of the *Mirati Sikandari* that the Sultan resolved to invade Mewar the next year but gave it up, as the Maharana sent his son with tribute and elephants, is only eyewash. The Sultan's resolution to invade Mewar the next year is inconsistent with the allegation that Malik Ayaz made peace as the Maharana offered submission. If the Maharana had agreed to pay tribute, the proper time for payment was when peace was made. Malik Ayaz would have brought it with the Maharana's son, and there was then no reason for any coldness towards the Malik, and no occasion for the people to call him a coward.

marched towards Idar.[1] He survived Bahadur Shah and died after A.D. 1543, and had the satisfaction of witnessing the beginning of the fall of the great enemy kingdom of Gujarāt.

The inherent strength of the Hindus enabled them to stand a temporary occupation of their country. They were never completely subdued or crushed. Mr. A. K. Forbes in his *Ras Mala*, says: "Whatever deeds of oppression and of blood may have been enacted at the time, and however the Muhammadan rulers may have chosen to believe, or the Muhammadan historians to represent the Hindus to be a crushed, subdued people, the fact remains beyond dispute that their descendants, in spite of many a subsequent danger, still possess the soil of which it was sought to deprive them; while little but squalid poverty and tottering ruins, represent the once proud sway of the dynasty of Shah Ahmad."[2]

---

[1] Forbes' *Ras Mala*, page 296.
[2] Forbes' *Ras Mala*, page 297.

CHAPTER X.

GUJARĀT PRINCES TAKE SHELTER WITH THE MAHARANA.

SULTAN Muzaffar Shah of Malwa had eight sons and two daughters. The eldest son, Sikandar Khan, was the legal heir to the throne and was liked by the Sultan, who had not much confidence in his other sons. The Sultan in his lifetime named Sikandar Khan as his successor, and gave suitable jagirs to the others. Bahadur Khan had a secret ambition to supplant his elder brother on the throne, and began to intrigue for it. He ingratiated himself into the favour of Shaikh Jiu, a Mussalman holy man, who lived at the tomb of Saint Kutabul Kutāb, near the prince's jagir, and who declared that the prince would some day be Sultan of Gujarāt. The pretensions of Bahadur Khan became known to the army and the nobles, and dissensions broke out between the two princes. Bahadur Khan, fearing the power of Sikandar Khan, determined to flee for safety. In answer to Shaikh Jiu's enquiry as to what else he desired besides the kingdom of Gujarāt, Bahadur Khan said that he was anxious to wrest the fort of Chitor from the Maharana to avenge what the Maharana had done after his conquest of Ahmadnagar, "when he slew so many Mussalmans and carried their women captive." The Shaikh became silent, but declared, on Bahadur's pressing for a reply, that the fall of Chitor was conditional on the Sultan's own destruction. Bahadur declared his willingness to undergo the sacrifice.[1]

In V. S. 1581 (1524 A. D.) Prince Bahadur fled from Gujarāt and took shelter with Maharana Sāngā at Chitor. He was not ashamed to ask for shelter and hospitality of the very man whose destruction he heartily desired and was secretly planning to

[1] Bayley's *Gujarāt*, page 305.

accomplish. The magnanimous Maharana, like the chivalrous Rajput that he was—unmindful of the political indiscretion of protecting enemies, disregarding the wise adage افعی کشتن و بچه اش نگاه داشتن کار خردمندان نیست (to kill the snake and to nurse its young one is not the act of a wise man)—received the prince "with kindness and showed him all attention." So much kindness was shown to him that the Maharana's mother used to call him "son." It is related that one day a nephew of the Maharana entertained Bahadur Khan at a banquet. While nautch was going on one of the dancing girls attracted Bahadur's attention by her singular beauty and exquisite dancing. Bahadur advanced nearer and nearer to look at her, when the host enquired if he recognised her. Bahadur Khan said "No," and asked who she was. The host replied that she was the daughter of the *qazi* of Ahmadnagar, that when the town was sacked, the *qazi* was killed and his women and daughters were carried off by the Rajputs. Bahadur Khan, on hearing this, flew into a rage and attacked and killed the Maharana's nephew. The Rajputs surrounded Bahadur and would have hacked him to pieces, but the Maharana's mother saved him by sending word to the Rajputs not to injure him.[1] The Maharana forgave the prince, but finding that he was disliked by the people, Bahadur left Chitor and went away towards Mewat.

Sultan Muzaffar Shah died in S. 1582 (A.D. 1526),[2] and was succeeded by his eldest son Sikandar Khan. During the protracted illness of Muzaffar Shah, the two parties in the army, headed respectively by Sikandar Khan and the Sultan's third son Latif Khan, contended for supremacy, and on Sikandar finally ascending the throne, Latif Khan and his younger brother Chand Khan, fled for protection to the Maharana. Sikandar Khan sent one Malik Latif, on whom he conferred the title of Sharza Khan, with an army to capture them. As the

[1] Bayley's *History of Gujarāt*, p. 305.
[2] Ibid, p. 307.

two princes were in the Maharana's protection the Maharana sent a sardar to drive Malik Latif out of Mewar. Latif "sustained a complete defeat." He was killed in action, while his troops lost no less than 1,700 men, the rest fleeing to Gujarāt.[1]

Mewar was now at the meridian of her greatness and prosperity. The greater part of Malwa had been conquered and incorporated with Mewar. Ranthambhore, Gagrone, Kalpi, Bhilsa and Chanderi were under the sway of the Maharana. Ajmer had been taken and Abu reduced, and Sāngā's governors administered both districts. Sāngā reduced to submission the Khanzādas of Mewat. The kings of Gwalior, Amber and Marwar acknowledged his supremacy and accompanied him in his wars as vassals or allies with their contingents. Maharana Sāngā had pushed back the Sultan of Delhi and made the *Peela khal,* near Agra, the northern boundary of his empire. Gujarāt had been plundered and then relinquished. The

[1] Brigg's Ferishta, Vol. IV, page 99.

three Sultans on the north, south and west, Sultans of Delhi, Malwa and Gujarāt, were all defeated and kept within their bounds. The song, the first two verses of which are given below, gives the popular view of the situation.[1]

According to the records of Devidan, the *Barwa* of the Mewar royal family, the Maharana had as many as 28 queens,[2] by whom he had seven sons and four

(१) इब्राहीम पूरब दिशा न उलटे,
पच्छम मुदाफर न दे पयाण ।
दखणी महमदशाह न दौड़े,
बाधो दामण त्रहूं सुरताण ॥ १ ॥

(On the east (of Mewar) Ibrahim (Lodi) cannot advance: Muzaffar (of Gujarāt) cannot come towards the west: Mahmud Shah (Khilji) cannot move towards the south (of Mewar); in this way, Maharana Sāngā has bound the feet of the three Sultans, *vide Maharana Yash Parakash*, by T. Bhur Singh, page 65.

[2] According to Barwā Debidān's records the queens of Maharana Sāngā were:—(1) Lakhu, daughter of Hada Rao Narbad Singh. (2) Karmetan, daughter of Hada Rao Narbad Singh. (3) Brajbai, daughter of Rāthor Jodhaji. (4) Bālkanwar, daughter of Rao Bharmalji. (5) Shyamkanwar, daughter of Hada Parbat Singhji. (6) Rajkanwar, daughter of Rao Ram Singhji Kherād. (7) Paipkanwar, daughter of Hada Rudra Bhanji. (8) Padamkanwar, daughter of Deora Abhai Singhji.

daughters. The eldest son, Bhojraj, who had married the celebrated Miran Bai,[1] daughter of Ratan Singh, younger brother of Viramdeva, Rao of Merta, died during his father's lifetime.

(9) Piarkanwar, daughter of Binai Singhji Rāthor. (10) Rambākanwar, daughter of Chandji Tuar. (11) Dhankanwar, daughter of Rao Bhanji, son of Rao Siyaji. (12) Kanwarābai, daughter of Rai Malji Solanki. (13) Ghansukhdé, daughter of Chauhan Kharagsénji. (14) Sawarbai, daughter of Hada Barjangji. (15) Gawarādé daughter of Gopji Deora. (16) Karmetān, daughter of Chauhan Shiv Singhji of Vāgadh. (17) Sultandé, daughter of Solanki Ridhmalji. (18) Ramkanwarbai, daughter of Sānklā Jodhsinghji. (19) Rajkanwar, daughter of Hāda Akhairajji. (20) Ramkanwar, daughter of Rao Nathji Solanki. (21) Ramkanwar, daughter of Mota Raja, Sankla. (22) Bhagwatkanwar, daughter of Solanki Abraji. (23) Kumkumkanwar, daughter of Hada Madho Singhji. (24) Padamkanwar, daughter of Solanki Rao Sursén. (25) Lalkanwar, daughter of Chauhan Jugmalji. (26) Raikanwar, daughter of Chauhan Man Singhji. (27) Karmetānbai, daughter of Rao Surji Rāthor of Chavad. (28) Lādkanwarbai, daughter of Rao Bhan of Idar.

Maharana Sāngā's sons were:—(1) Bhojraj, (2) Karan Singh, (3) Ratan Singh, (4) Parvat Singh, (5) Krishnadas, (6) Vikramaditya, (7) Udai Singh.

[1] Col. Tod has stated Miran Bai to be the queen of Kumbha. This is an error. Kumbha was killed in S. 1524 (A.D. 1467), while Miran's grandfathar, Duda, became Raja of Merta after that year. Miran's father, Ratan Singh, was killed in the battle of Khanua 59 years after Kumbha's death, and her cousin Jaimal at Chitor during Akbar's attack, 99 years after Kumbha's death. Miran Bai was married to Prince Bhojraj in S. 1573

Sāngā's second son Ratan Singh, by Queen Dhankanwar, daughter of Prince Bagha, eldest son of Rao Suja of Mewar, was now the heir-apparent. Amongst Sāngā's queens were two daughters of Bhanda's son Narbad Hādā, Raja of Bundi. By the second of these, Karmetan, Sāngā had two sons, Vicramaditya and Udai Singh. Karmetan enjoyed the confidence and affection of Sāngā in a special degree. Solicitous of her sons' welfare, she begged the Maharana to make provision for them, and suggested that the fort and pargannah of Ranthambhore night be given to them as jagir. The Maharana granted the request. The Hadi queen, knowing well that without proper support, the boys would not be able to keep that stronghold, requested that Hada Suraj Mal, her brother, who was one of the bravest and most important chiefs at the time, might be appointed their guardian to protect them and their estate. The Maharana announced

(A.D. 1516). Miran Bai was born about S. 1555 (A.D. 1498) and died in S. 1603 (A.D. 1546) at Dwarka (Kathiawar), at which holy place she had been residing for several years. *Vide Chaturkula Charitra* (History of the Rāthor family of Merta) and *Vir Vinod.*

the grant in open Darbar the next day, and asked Suraj Mal to accept the responsible position. Suraj Mal said that he was a vassal of the empire, and his fidelity to the throne forbade his committing himself to a course of conduct inconsistent with his loyalty to the throne of Chitor. The matter was then referred to the heir-apparent to the throne, Prince Ratan Singh. He, out of deference to the wishes of his father Maharana Sāngā, gave his consent to the proposal, on which Suraj Mal took the hands of both the young princes in his own, as well as the *patta* of Ranthambhore, in token of his acceptance of the responsible position assigned to him. This impolitic proceeding on the part of Queen Karmetan sowed dissension among the nobility of Mewar, and was, as later events proved, one of the causes of the fall of Chitor. This is one of the many instances which abound in Indian history to prove the fatal consequences of polygamy in the royal houses of the Hindus.

CHAPTER XI.

Bābur.

While the Pathan power in India was tottering to its fall, there appeared in Kabul a man of extraordinary ability and character, who was destined to found one of the greatest kingdoms of medieval times. That man was Zahiruddin Muhammad Bābur. Bābur was born in the purple and belonged to a family which had long ruled in Central Asia. The Chaghtai Turks,[1] up to Amir Taraghyan, were Buddhists in faith. Taraghyan was the first to embrace Islam. He was the father of the celebrated Timur, or Tamerlane, who was born of Nagina Khatun on 25 Shaban H. 736 (10th April A.D. 1336), at Sabz or Kesh,

[1] Colonel Tod thinks that there are grounds to assert that the Chaghtai Turks were a branch of the Yadava Rajput tribe to which the Jaisalmer family belongs.

30 miles from Samarkand. Tamerlane became Amir of Bokhara on 10th April A.D. 1370. He conquered Persia, a part of Arabia and Mesopotamia. In A.D. 1398 he invaded India, took and plundered Delhi, and returned home laden with rich booty. He died at Atrar, 76 miles from Samarkand, on 19th February 1405 A.D. He was a great tyrant, and his oppressions and depredations are matters of history. He was succeeded by his son, Miran Shah, whose sixth son, Sultan Mahmud Mirza, on his deathbed placing his son Abu Sayid's hands in those of Ulugh Beg, son of Mirza Shah Rukh, a grandson of Timur, ruler of Khorasan, recommended him to Ulugh Khan's protection.[1] Abu Sayid was born in A.D. 1427 and became king of Turkistan and Afghanistan at the age of 25. On 5 February 1469 he became a prisoner in a battle against Uzan Husain, a Turkoman Chief, and was put to death three days later. His fourth son, Umar Shaikh Mirza, born in A.D. 1456,

[1] Abu Sayid repaid the kindness and generosity of Ulugh Beg by treachery.

inherited the small kingdom of Ferghana, and continued to rule it till 10 June A.D. 1494, when he was killed by the fall of a house while amusing himself with his tame pigeons in his palace, which stood on an eminence in the castle of Akhsi. The pigeon-house stood on the edge of a steep cliff overhanging the river below. Its foundations gave way, and he was precipitated down the cliff along with the building and killed on the spot.[1] Umar Shaikh left three sons, the eldest Zahiruddin Muhammad Bābur, and the second Jahangir Mirza. The third, Nasir Mirza, was by a concubine.

Zahiruddin Muhammad Bābur was born on 6 Muharrum, H. 888 (15th February, A.D. 1483). His mother, Kutlak Nigār Khānam, was the second daughter of Yunis Khan, the grand Khan of the Moghuls, who was a descendant of Changez Khan.[2] On

1 Erskine's *History of India*, Vol. I, p. 78.

2 Bābur's genealogy on the father's side was: Bābur, son of Umar Shaikh Mirza, son of Abu Sayid Mirza, the son of Muhammad Mirza, the son of Miran Shah, the son of Amir Timur Korkān. On his mother's side,

11 June 1494, at the age of 11, Bābur became ruler of Ferghana, on the death of his father.

At his birth he was named Zahiruddin Muhammad by Khwāja Nasiruddin Abdulla, the celebrated spiritual guide in Transoxiana. The Chaghtais finding it difficult to pronounce the Arabic word Zahiruddin, called him Bābur, which his parents adopted.

The kingdom of Ferghana, now Kokān, is surrounded on all sides by mountains, some of which are covered with perpetual snow. The capital, Andejān, with its important fortress, is situated to the south of the river Sirr or Sehun. Umar Shaikh, however, used to live in Akhsi, the second important town of the kingdom, as its fortress was the strongest in the kingdom. Ferghana possesses a rich soil and lies in a

it was: Kutlak Nigār Khānam, daughter of Yunis Khan, the son of Weis Khan, the son of Sher Ali Khan, the son of Muhammad Khwaja, the son of Khizr Khwaja, the son of Tughlak Timur, the son of Isan Bugha, the son of Dawa Chichan, the son of Borak Khan, the son of Sukar, the son of Kamgar, the son of Chaghtai, the son of the famous Changez Khan.

temperate climate, though exposed to violent heat in summer and severe cold in winter. It abounds in corn and fruits, specially the peach, the pomegranate, the almond and melon. Its orchards and gardens were celebrated in olden days.

Bābur describes his father as a brave, good-humoured prince of a sweet temper, elegant and refined in his manners and conversation, fond of letters, and remarkable for his justice. In his external policy he was ambitious, restless and unsteady. At the time of Umar Shaikh's death, his elder brother, Sultan Ahmad Mirza, King of Samarkand, and Sultan Mirza his brother-in-law, having combined to deprive Umar Shaikh of his little kingdom, were marching from north and south, and it was with difficulty and after some fighting that Bābur's nobles extricated the principality from this danger. At 15 years of age, Bābur took Samarkand in November A.D. 1497. Samarkand was one of the most celebrated and populous cities at the time. It had been the capital of Tamerlane the Great. Bābur found the city worn out from the long continuance of the blockade; and the surrounding country had been laid waste by hostile armies for two successive summers. His followers began to desert him and return home. A party headed by Azan Hasan and Tambal, demanded that Bābur having taken Samarkand, should give Andejan and Akhsi to his younger brother, Jahangir Mirza. Bābur refused the demand, upon which Jahangir besieged Andejan. Bābur was seriously ill at the time. On his recovery, he abandoned Samarkand to relieve Andejan. On the way he learnt that Andejan had been surrendered the day he had left Samarkand. Bābur says in his memoirs: "To save Andejan, I had given up Samarkand, and now found that I had lost the one without preserving the other." He was left without a country and without followers. He says: "I became a prey to vexation and melancholy, for since I had been a sovereign prince, I never before had been separated in this manner from my country and followers; and since the day I had known myself, I had never experienced such care and suffering." Bābur now resolved to instigate his maternal uncle, Sultan Mahmud Khan, to take Andejan. Sultan Mahmud, ever ready to go where a country was to be plundered, marched towards Andejan, but Jahangir Mirza's men persuaded him to return to his country. Bābur's situation became more desperate than ever. "I was now reduced to a very distressed situation," says he, "and wept a great deal." A second attempt on Samarkand with Sultan Mahmud's assistance having failed, Bābur repaired to the court of his uncle, and persuaded him to give him assistance. He took Nasukh, but abandoned it and returned to Khojend. His old servant Ali Dost, sent for Bābur and gave up to him Marghinan. Azan Hasan attempted to drive Bābur out of Marghinan but failed. Bābur advanced and took Andejan. The Moghuls, however, revolted and defeated Bābur. Eventually a peace was made, by which the kingdom was partitioned between Bābur and Jahangir Mirza, in February 1500 A.D., and it was stipulated that both should attack Samarkand, and should they succeed, Bābur should keep it and give up Andejan to Jahangir Mirza. The direction of Bābur's affairs was in the hands of Mir Ali Dost, a Moghul, who removed Bābur's favourites one after another from the little Court. Ali Dost and his son were the real rulers of the little State. Bābur says: "My situation was singularly delicate, and I was forced to be silent. Many were the indignities which I endured at that time, both from father and son." Bābur, at the invitation of Muhammad Mazid Tarkhan, marched to take Samarkand. No sooner had Bābur started on this expedition than Tambol's brother Khalil, attacked the fortress of Ush and took it from Bābur's garrison. And when Bābur reached Yuratkhan, five miles from Samarkand, news reached him that the powerful Shaibani Khan, the Uzbek Chief of Turkistan, was in full march towards that city. Bābur broke up the blockade of Samarkand, and instead of falling back on his hereditary dominions, now in the hands of his hereditary enemies, he marched towards Kesh. Here he learnt of the surrender of Samarkand; and Muhammad Mazid and other Begs separating from him,

Bābur was left with few adherents, and "once more felt himself in a most destitute and wretched situation, without army or country or home. He knew not which way to turn." Bābur thought of migrating to the remoter wilds of Tartary, but eventually made up his mind to return towards Samarkand and meet whatever fortune awaited him there. With the greatest difficulty he traversed the pass of Sir-e-tāk and came to Kān. At a little distance from Samarkand Kamber Ali joined Bābur. Shaibani was encamped with seven or eight thousand men near Khwaja Didār and had a garrison of five or six hundred men in Samarkand. Mehdi Sultan and other adherents of Shaibani, with two thousand men, were encamped near by. Bābur with all his exertions could not muster more than 240 followers. None but a man of the most heroic ardour would have ventured to think of extricating himself from his difficulties except by retreat. Bābur saw that if he had any chance of retrieving his affairs it could only be by bold measures, and he resolved to surprise Samarkand, which daring enterprise offered the best prospect of success. The first attempt failed, but the second succeeded beyond his expectations. The people, tired of the barbarous Uzbeks, hailed Bābur with joy. Shaibani galloped up to the town with a few followers at daybreak, but finding it in Bābur's possession and the whole population against himself, retired towards Bokhara. Bābur was at the time of this heroic enterprise in his eighteenth year. Though Bābur obtained Samarkand, Shaibani Khan's power was unbroken. In a few months he advanced from Bokhara and took the fort of Dabusi by storm and put Bābur's garrison to the sword. Bābur left Samarkand to take the field against him (about May 1501 A.D.) Shaibani planned a night attack which failed. Bābur divided his army into four divisions, consisting of right and left wings, centre and advance, and marched forward. The enemy was ready to receive Bābur. Bābur's left was turned. The enemy then attacked his centre in the rear and threw his army into confusion. Bābur sustained a complete defeat. Only 10 or 15 men remained round him. Bābur fled, and after crossing the river

Kohik, reached Samarkand, which Shaibani lost no time in investing. After several months' blockade, Bābur capitulated, one of the articles of the treaty being the marriage of Bābur's sister, Khanzada Begum, with Shaibani—"part of the price paid for his unmolested escape." Thus Samarkand was again lost in September 1501 A.D. Bābur, now in his nineteenth year, driven from Samarkand, made for Ilan-uti. After great sufferings and privations and a stunning fall from his horse, Bābur reached Dizak, where he had meat and bread and fruit to eat. He says in his memoirs: "In my whole life, I never enjoyed myself so much." "It has been my lot," he adds, "four or five times in the course of my life, to pass in a similar manner from distress and suffering to enjoyment and ease, but this was the first time I had ever been so circumstanced, and most keenly did I feel the transition from the injuries of my enemy and the gnawings of absolute hunger, to the charms of security and the delights of the plenty."[1]

[1] Erskine's *History of India*, Vol. I, p. 159.

Bābur repaired to his uncle Sultan Mahmud, who assigned the district of Dehkāt to him. Here Bābur lived in the house of one of the headmen of the place and had often to go about bare-footed. The aged mother of the chief told Bābur stories of the wonderful land of India which she had heard from one of her relations who had accompanied Timur when he invaded Hindustan. These stories concerning the wonders of India, probably fired Bābur's youthful imagination and implanted in him an ardent desire to visit that distant land.

From Dehkāt, Bābur sent a cap for his brother, Jehangir Mirza, and a sword to Tambal. Tired of "the unsettled way of living and with having no house or home, life became a burden to" Bābur, who preferred "to live unknown and undistinguished into some corner than continue to drag on existence in wretchedness and misery," which he then endured. Bābur's uncle soon had occasion to attack Tambal, and Bābur with a part of his army took Ush and advanced on Andejan. He was, however, surprised by Tambal. Bābur was wounded by an arrow, which pierced his right thigh; while Tambal riding up discharged full on his head a furious sabre blow which stunned him. The sword was the one which Bābur had presented him. The steel cap saved Bābur, but his head was bruised. Another sabre stroke fell on his quiver, and Bābur, to save himself, fled. He went to Akhsi, but was driven away from there. With 20 or 30 men he fled, pursued by the enemy. All his followers were left behind one after another, and at length Bābur was left alone. Two of his enemy were gaining upon him. When they came within bowshot, they called out to him to stop, and swore that they meant no harm to him. All three passed the night in the hills. Bābur was eventually discovered there. He was told that Tambal wanted to make him king. Bābur disbelieved the story and retired to spend the few moments yet left him in religious meditations and in preparation for the next world. He, however, managed to escape, and joined the Moghul khans, who were marching against Ferghana. Shaibani, however, surprised them and made the khans his prisoners, Bābur escaping (June 1503) to the southern hills of Ferghana. Bābur was compelled to wander as a fugitive and an outlaw in the hilly country, accompanied by his mother and some followers. After he had been subjected for a year to the utmost extremes of hardship and suffering, hunted from village to village and from forest to mountain, finding the toils of his pursuers closing around him, and seeing that his partisans were totally dispersed and not a chance of success was left, he held a consultation with his small but devoted band. Their prospects were dreary and dark, and opposition to Shaibani was hopeless. He could not expect long to secure even his life, if he continued to roam as an adventurer in a territory which he had once vainly called his own. Young as he was, the world was before him. He therefore resolved to abandon for a time his native country and to court success in foreign lands. Accordingly, in the summer of H. 910 (A.D. 1504), Bābur bade a last adieu to his native land, and the whole party set out to cross the lofty and snow-covered range of mountains that separate Andejan from Karatagin and Hissar.

Bābur was joined by many people on the way, and as he marched through the territories of Khusrau Shah, who ruled from Karatagin to Hindukush and Balkh to Badakhshan, Khusrau's brother Baki Chaghaniani, joined Bābur. In a few days all his followers came to Bābur, who now resolved to conquer Kabul. The city surrendered after a siege of only a few days in October 1504 A.D. Thus Bābur little more than three months after leaving, as a houseless exile, his little kingdom of Ferghana, saw himself sovereign of the far more extensive and powerful kingdoms of Kabul and Ghazni.

Bābur had been in Kabul but a short time when Yar Muhammad, a son of Daria Khan of Bhera, a district lying beyond the Indus on the south of Jhelum, invited him to that country. Bābur thereupon resolved on an incursion into India. He set out from Kabul in Shaban H. 910 (January 1505), and reached Jalalabad in six days, and traversing the Khaibar Pass proceeded to Bekram, now Peshawar. After a consultation, the plan of crossing the Indus was abandoned, and the army was led on a marauding expedition to Kohat, Bannu, Bangash and Dasht Damān. Passing by a small dependency of Multan, Bābur went on to Ghazni and returned to Kabul in four months.

In the meantime, Shaibani laid siege to Balkh, and its ruler, Sultan Husain Mirza, invited Bābur to assist him to repel the invasion. Bābur consented and left Kabul. But Balkh fell before Bābur reached there. Bābur, therefore, after visiting Herat, set out in December 1506 A.D., on the return journey to Kabul, where an insurrection had taken place in his absence. He had taken Kandahar and bestowed it on his brother Nasir Mirza, when Shaibani Khan advanced rapidly in the hope of surprising him there. Finding Bābur gone towards Kabul, he invested Kandahar. This so alarmed Bābur, and such was the wholesome fear inspired by the prowess and talents of Shaibani, that at a council held to decide what course to adopt in this difficult emergency, it was considered hopeless even to attempt the defence of the country of Kabul, and it was decided to make an inroad into India to escape the tempest. Leaving Kabul under the charge of Abdul Razzak, the late king, Bābur marched down the Kabul river for the Indus. The intervening passes were in the possession of Afghan tribes, who are robbers even in peace times. Bābur thus speaks of their attitude: "When they understood that I had abandoned Kabul and was marching for Hindustan, their usual insolence was increased tenfold." Bābur showed fight and the Afghans dispersed. He arrived at Adinapur, now Jalalabad. From here he sent four divisions to plunder the country around and waited for news from Kabul. He soon heard that Kandahar had fallen, that it was given back to the Arghuns and that Nasir Mirza was allowed to depart to Ghazni. Hearing also that Shaibani had returned to Turkistan to quell trouble at home, Bābur returned to Kabul and assumed the title of *Padshah*. Even here he got no rest. His Moghul army, to which he owed the throne of Kabul, revolted, and it was with the greatest difficulty that he defeated the rebel Moghul chiefs (A.D. 1508) and gained success over them—a success to achieve which his bodily strength and personal gallantry contributed not a little. "His heroism and desperation appalled his enemies and reanimated his followers."

Bābur now enjoyed repose for two years. He then heard of the victory gained by the King of Persia, Shah Ismail Safvi, over Shaibani Khan at Merv.[1] Khan Mirza sent the welcome news by a messenger, who travelled post haste to inform Bābur of the momentous happenings in the north and invited him to recover his patrimony. Bābur started, and meeting with

[1] Shaibani's end was very inglorious. Defeated in battle at Mahmudabad of Merv he took shelter with 500 men in an inclosure, and when pressed hard they all jumped over the wall to escape towards the river, but in doing so fell in heaps on each other. Shaibani was overlaid and smothered by the crowd after him. His body was unearthed and his head was cut off and presented to Shah Ismail. The skin of his head was stuffed with hay and sent to Sultan Bayazid, the Turkish Emperor of Constantinople. The skull, set in gold, was made into a drinking cup, which the Shah was proud of displaying at his great entertainments.

little opposition, recovered Samarkand and Bokhara. His dominions now extended from the deserts of Tartary to the limits of Ghazni, and comprehended Kabul, Ghazni, Kunduz, Hissar, Samarkand, Bokhara Ferghana, Tashkand and Seiram. Kabul and Ghazni he gave to Nasir Mirza, himself taking up his residence at Samarkand. Bābur was now in his 29th year (1511-12 A.D.).

Like his two previous conquests of Samarkand, this third one was also of short duration. Bābur had relied chiefly on the assistance of the Shah of Persia for his success in Transoxiana, and he now adopted the Persian dress and issued an order to his troops to do the same, particularly the Persian cap. This alienated the sympathies of the people, who were orthodox Sunnies, and a storm of the Uzbeks gathering beyond the Sirr soon poured down in all its fury on the plains of Bokhara. Bābur was driven from Samarkand. He defended himself at Hissar and sent for assistance to Shah Ismail, who sent an army under Amir

Nijm Sani to assist Bābur. Though Amir Nijm gained a few successes, he was defeated with great slaughter at Ghazhdewan, and Bābur lost all hope of again ascending the throne of Samarkand and Bokhara. Hissar, too, was taken by the Uzbeks and Bābur again crossed the Hindukush and returned to Kabul towards the end of 1513 or early in 1514 A.D. Nasir Mirza at once yielded Kabul to him, himself retiring to his old government of Ghazni. Bābur now enjoyed some years of peace, which he employed in settling the government of his kingdom and reducing to submission the various mountain tribes on every side.

In 1519 A.D., Bābur invaded a part of the Panjab, and in 1520 he again entered the Panjab and advanced as far as Sialkot, when he was recalled by an invasion of Kabul. He now resolved to take and incorporate Kandahar with his dominions, preliminary to his invasion of India. He besieged Kandahar, which was ably defended by its ruler, Shah Beg. In A.D. 1522, however, it was finally surrendered to him.

CHAPTER XII.

Sāngā and Bābur.

The accession of Sultan Ibrahim Lodi to the throne of Delhi in A.D. 1517, showed the weak points of the Afghan Sultanate of Hindustan, which was a congeries of several virtually independent Pathan principalities and jagirs.

The cruelty of Ibrahim filled his reign with rebellions by the nobles of the kingdom. The Sultan possessed neither the tact to control them, nor the ability to crush them. At length, Daulat Khan Lodi, the governor of Lahore, invited Bābur, the king of Kabul, to take possession of Hindustan. Bābur had ere this made unsuccessful attempts to take the Panjab. He says in his autobiography that Maharana Sāngā had also sent him a message to the effect that should he (Bābur) advance and take Delhi, he (Sāngā) would take Agra from the Lodi king.

Finding the circumstances favourable, Bābur left Kabul, took a part of the Panjab and advanced towards Delhi. Circumstances, however, soon afterwards obliged him to return to Kabul.

In the meantime the dissensions in the Afghan kingdom of Delhi increased and prince Alauddin, known as Alam Khan, the uncle of Sultan Ibrahim Lodi, repaired to Kabul and induced Bābur to help him to the throne of Delhi, promising him in lieu of his assistance, the whole of the Panjab. Alam Khan returned to India and, aided by Bābur's generals in the Panjab, advanced towards Delhi, but was defeated and put to flight by Sultan Ibrahim. Bābur, however, perceiving the time favourable for his designs, as Hindustan was torn asunder by hopeless dissensions and rivalries, crossed the Indus with only 12,000 men, which swelled to about seventy thousand when he came face to face with the Sultan of Delhi on the celebrated field of Panipat, where the sovereignty of Hindustan has been so often lost and won. After waiting for a few days, during which intrigue was not idle, Bābur made dispositions for a battle, which took place on 29 April 1526 A.D. The Delhi army was defeated and the Sultan lost his life. A week after this, Bābur was crowned king at Delhi and the *khutba* was read in his name.

After waiting a few months to see if Sāngā moved towards Agra, he advanced and took possession of it. Agra was then only an appanage of Byana, which was a place of great strategical and political importance. Byana had fallen into the hands of the Maharana after the defeat of Ibrahim, and its ruler, Nizam Khan, was a vassal of Mewar.

Bābur, however, knew very well that Ibrahim was not his most formidable opponent in India. He was aware of the great power and prestige of Maharana Sāngā and knew that with him as a neighbour, his throne stood on very slender support. He, therefore, began to take steps to secure Byana. Nizam Khan wished to play Bābur and Sāngā against each other. He told Bābur that he was a vassal of Sāngā, and when Sāngā called him to his duty he excused himself by saying that Bābur would not allow him to do so. As Byana belonged by right to Sāngā, he resolved to march against Nizam Khan to enforce obedience. Bābur wishing to forestall Sāngā, sent an army under Tardi Beg to take it. Alim Khan, brother of Nizam Khan, also joined the Turks. Bābur's army was, however, defeated and put to flight by Nizam Khan. But when Sāngā advanced from Ranthambhore, Nizam Khan finding it impossible to hold Byana against the Maharana, voluntarily surrendered the stronghold to Bābur,[1] receiving in return a jagir in the Doab. Bābur's occupation of Byana was an open attack on the territory of the Maharana, and the Maharana regarding this as a challenge, took up the gauntlet and began to make preparations to drive out the Turks from Hindustan.

Nizam Khan's action brought Sāngā and Bābur face to face earlier than Bābur

[1] Erskine's *History of India*, Vol. I, pp. 452-53.

wished. Bābur was yet more or less of a stranger to Hindustan and he wished to consolidate his power and position by reducing to submission the various Pathan Chiefs and semi-independent Afghan governors of different provices of Hindustan before engaging in a war with Sāngā, which Bābur knew very well would mean the latter's sovereignty of Hindustan or a final defeat of all his hopes and ambitions.

Sāngā and Bābur are the two outstanding personalities of the time in India. Though Sāngā was no ordinary Rajput king, Bābur was an equally remarkable personality. Both were of about the same age. Sāngā was born in A.D. 1482 and Bābur in A.D. 1483. Both were men of valour and had received their training in the school of adversity. The early life of Bābur had been a continuous record of trouble, disappointment and defeat; but of unremitting toil, ever-renewed effort, unflagging energy, great personal bravery and confidence. He had met with so many ups and downs in his life that he never lost courage, and was always prepared for difficulties and disappointments. His career was passed amongst the barbarians of the North, the rugged, turbulent and treacherous tribes of Turkistan and Transoxiana; and his hardy constitution, his indomitable courage, his varied experience, and his great knowledge of men, stood him in good stead when he was opposed by the chivalry of Rajputana—a country far in advance of Central Asia in humanity and culture.

Bābur was a man of amiable disposition, and was of a joyous nature. He was fond of the good things of life. He had some learning and culture and was not devoid of generous instincts when political considerations did not come into play. As a man and a leader he was head and shoulders above the chieftains and nobles who followed his fortunes in India. He was Maharana Sāngā's equal in courage and determination and not inferior to him in personal valour. And if he was inferior to the Maharana in chivalry, heroism, generosity,[1] highmindedness and devotion to

[1] Not only did Sāngā generously bestow Mandu on the defeated Sultan Mahmud, but gave away Chitor to

the dictates of honour, he was his superior in circumspection, perseverance, judgment, and above all, in quickness to take advantage of every occasion favourable to him. Defeat after defeat, disaster following disaster made Bābur wideawake, circumspect and artful. They matured his judgment, gave him a richer knowledge of human nature and prepared him to meet all emergencies. On the other hand, unbroken success after coming to the throne, victory following victory, gave Sāngā self-confidence, courage and hope, enhanced his prestige and glory, but made him minimize difficulties and neglect taking proper precautions. It impaired his power of properly appreciating the meaning and the bearing of incidents and attendant

the Kesaria Charan Haridas after the victory over Mahmud Khilji. Haridas, however, presented the fortress again to the Maharana. The following verses by Haridas are extant in Rajputana :

मांडवगढ़ गज्जर घरहुके
रेणवां दीध चत्रगढ़राण

Thou, O! Rana, didst allow the kings of Mandu and Gujarāt to return home, and gavest away the fortress of Chitor to Renwa Charan.

Also दिध चित्रकोट कवियां छुमाया,
दिन चिजड़ै में रीझदिया ॥

circumstances on the success of a plan. While Sāngā was a greater hero and a more chivalrous leader of men, Bābur was a greater politician and a more wary and skilful general. While Sāngā had prestige, bravery, dash, and numbers on his side, Bābur had artfulness, desperation and religious fervour to support him.

CHAPTER XIII.

WAR WITH BĀBUR. BATTLE OF KHANUĀ.

In his expedition against Bābur, Sāngā received assistance from an unexpected quarter. After the fall of the Lodi dynasty, the Afghan chiefs who exercised supreme power in Hindustan became apprehensive of losing their position of influence and power, when they saw that, unlike Timur, Bābur intended to stay in India and found a kingdom on the ruins of the Afghan power. They, therefore, combined and began to devise means to drive the Turks out of India. As, however, Bābur held Delhi and Agra, the eastern Afghans rallied round the standard of Bābur Khan Lohani, whom they raised to the throne of Behar under the name of Sultan Muhammad Shah.[1] The Western Afghan Confederacy, headed by Nawab Hasan Khan of Mewat, who ruled

1 Erskine's *History of India*, Vol. I, p. 443.

at Alwar, espoused the cause of Mahmud Lodi, a brother of Sultan Ibrahim. The confederates appealed to the Maharana to drive the Turks out of India. They acknowledged him as their suzerain and promised to govern the country occupied by them as his feudatories.

Bābur, who had sent Humayun against the Eastern Afghan Confederacy, on hearing that Sāngā was preparing an army to march against Byana, wrote to Humayun to return with all available troops to Agra. Humayun not meeting with strong opposition in the east, after taking Jaunpur, returned to Agra and joined Bābur.

Afraid of the great power of Sāngā, Bābur now wished to conciliate the western Afghans, and in order to gain over their leader, Hasan Khan of Mewat, released his son Naharkhan, who had been taken prisoner at Panipat after the defeat of Ibrahim Lodi. Bābur sent him to his father with a dress of honour and an earnest request to espouse his cause.

Muhammad Zeitun and Tatarkhan Sarangkhani were won over. They surrendered the forts of Dholpur and Gwalior to Bābur and were given jagirs in other places. All these chieftains now came to Bābur with their armies.

On 11th February A.D. 1527, Bābur marched out of Agra to proceed against Sāngā but halted a few days near the town to collect his troops and get his artillery in order. He advanced to Medhakur, where he had previously had wells dug for water, and the next day to Fatehpur Sikri, where he encamped and began to fortify his position.

Maharana Sāngā started from Chitor with a large army in Baisakh S. 1584.[1] Prince Mahmud Khan Lodi who had taken shelter with the Maharana, was also in the Maharana's army in the hope of recovering the kingdom lost by his brother Ibrahim Lodi. When news of the Maharana's arrival at Ranthambhore reached Bābur he became

[1] *Chatur Kula Charitra*, p. 26.

alarmed, for he knew that Sāngā, as he says in his Memoirs, was a very powerful king, and that "the high eminence he then held, he had attained by his valour and his sword." He knew very well that the Afghan chiefs in India were all at heart his enemies. He therefore made overtures for peace through Raja Silhiddi Tuar of Raisen, a feudatory of the Maharana, but the Maharana rejected the overtures, and after taking the strong fort of Kandar from Hasan Makan,[1] who in vain applied to Bābur for help, advanced to Byana. Hasan Khan of Mewat who, along with other chieftains "looked to Sāngā for aid," did not take the bait offered by Bābur through Nahar Khan, but joined Sāngā with ten thousand horse. The Maharana attacked and took Byana, the governor, Mehdi Khwaja, fleeing to Bābur with the remnant of his troops. The Maharana's army advanced and fell on Bābur's advanced guard on 21st February 1527 (Chaitra Bad 6th, S. 1583 = 20

[1] Erskine's *History of India*, Vol. I., p. 448.

Jamadi ul Avval H. 933). This advanced guard was "entirely destroyed, the fugitives carrying to the main body the accounts of the disaster, which paralysed their energies, and made them entrench for security instead of advancing with the confidence of victory. Reinforcements met the same fate and were pursued to the camp." [1]

Mr. Erskine says: "They had had some sharp encounters with the Rajputs, in which they had been severely handled and taught to respect their new enemy. A party from the garrison had some days before incautiously advanced too far from the fort, when the Rajputs fell upon them and drove them in. All the troops engaged in this affair united in bestowing unbounded praise on the gallantry and prowess of the enemy (Rajputs). Indeed the Jaghtai Turks found that they had now to contend with a foe more formidable than either the Afghans or any of the natives of India to whom they had yet been opposed. The Rajputs, energetic, chivalrous, fond of battle and

[1] Tod's *Rajasthan*, Vol. I., p. 303.

bloodshed, animated by strong national spirit and led on by a hero, were ready to meet, face to face, the boldest veterans of the camp, and were at all times prepared to lay down their life for their honour."

Mr. Stanley Lane Poole says: "Their chivalry and lofty sense of honour inspired nobler feats and sacrifices than any that were conceived by Bābur's less highly-wrought soldiers." [1]

Mir Abdul Aziz, who was in charge of the advance, had pickets pushed on for seven or eight miles. A body of Rajputs fell upon him and "many of his men were killed, others taken prisoners and carried off the field on the very first onset." "The minister's son, Mohib Ali Khalifa, pushed forward to his assistance, and numbers of separate horsemen, as fast as they were equipped, were sent off at the best of their speed. Mohib Ali found everything in disorder, Abdul Aziz's standard taken and many excellent officers slain. Not only was he unable to turn the

[1] Stanley Lane Poole's *Bābur*, p. 176.

tide of success but was himself unhorsed, though finally brought off by a desperate charge of his followers. Bābur's troops were then pursued for about two miles." [1]

To detach Hasan Khan Mewati from the Maharana, Bābur had sent a predatory force into Mewat with orders "to plunder the country, to carry off the inhabitants into captivity, and to leave nothing undone to ruin the province. The ravages were extended into many of the neighbouring districts, but the results of this diversion did not answer his expectations."

"The repeated successes of the Rajputs, the unexpected valour and good conduct they displayed, and their numbers, for they are said to have amounted to an hundred and twenty thousand horse, had begun to spread a visible discouragement among the troops."[2] Bābur again opened negotiations for peace, and employed the time thus gained to strengthen his position and give his men time to recover their confidence. In order

[1] Erskine's *History of India*, Vol. I, p. 465.
[2] Erskine's *History of India*, Vol. I, p. 465-6.

to reassure the drooping spirits of his troops, he threw up entrenchments, in which he placed his artillery, connecting his guns by chains, and in the more exposed parts, *chevaux de frise*, united by leather ropes. These operations were continued for 3 or 4 weeks, during which time the army remained blockaded in this encampment. About this time he received a reinforcement of 500 volunteers from Kabul, who were accompanied by a noted astrologer, Muhammad Sharif. Even the astrologer instead of being of assistance, "added to the depression and panic which prevailed in the camp by declaring his opinion that the planet Mars, being in the west, whoever engaged, coming from the opposite direction, would be defeated."[1]

Feelings of extreme uneasiness and dismay crowded the mind of Bābur when he was thus forcibly cooped up in his entrenched camp, while the Rajputs were in possession of the open country. His introspective spirit was quickened, and reviewing his past

[1] Erskine's *History of India*, Vol. I, p. 466.

life, he felt that he had grossly and openly violated one of the chief principles of his faith, being firmly addicted to drinking wine. He now determined "to renounce this besetting sin in order to merit superior aid to extricate him from his peril." Bābur says in his Memoirs: "On Monday, the 23rd of Jamadi ul Awwal, I had mounted to survey my posts, and in the course of my ride was seriously struck with the reflection that I had always resolved one time or another to make an effectual repentance, and that some traces of the hankering after a renunciation of forbidden works had ever remained in my heart: I said to myself:

'Oh my soul,
How long wilt thou continue to take pleasure in sin,
Repentence is not unpalatable—taste it.'

"Having withdrawn myself from such temptation, I vowed never more to drink wine. Having sent for the gold and silver goblets and cups, with all the other utensils used for drinking parties, I directed them to be broken, and renounced the use of wine, purifying my mind. The fragments of the goblets and other utensils of gold and silver

I directed to be divided amongst dervishes and the poor." Bābur also vowed not to cut the beard, but to allow it to grow like a true Mussalman. Nearly 300 of his men, great and small, made such vows of reformation.

"The dejection and alarm of Bābur's troops," says Erskine, "had at this time reached their extreme point. The contagion had infected even his highest officers." "The destruction of the wine flasks," says Tod, "would appear only to have added to the existing consternation." In his despair, as a last resort, Bābur determined to make an appeal to the religious feelings of his followers, "so powerful with all Moslems."

Bābur says in his Memoirs: "At this time, as I have already observed, in consequence of preceding events, a general consternation and alarm prevailed among the great and small. There was not a single person who uttered a manly word, nor an individual who delivered a courageous opinion. The Vaziers whose duty it was to give good counsel and the Amirs who enjoyed the wealth of kingdoms, neither spoke bravely nor was their counsel or deportment such as became men of firmness." "At length," continues Bābur, "observing the universal discouragement of my troops and their total want of spirit I came to a resolution. Having called a general assembly of my Amirs and officers, I addressed them: 'Noblemen and soldiers! Every man that cometh into this world is subject to dissolution. When *we* are passed away and gone God survives, One and Unchangeable. Whoever sits down to the feast of life must, before it is over, drink of the cup of death. He who arrives at the inn of mortality, the world, must one day, without fail, take his departure from that mansion of sorrow. How much better then is it to die with honour than to live with infamy.

> 'Give me but fame, and if I die I am contented,
> 'If fame be mine, let death claim my body.'

'The most High God has been propitious to us. He has now placed us in such a crisis that if we fall in the field we die the death of martyrs; if we survive, we rise victorious, the avengers of His sacred cause.

Let us, therefore, with one accord swear on God's holy word, that none of us will for a moment think of turning his face from this warfare; or shrink from the battle and slaughter that ensue, till his soul is separated from his body.' Master and servant, small and great, all with emulation seizing the blessed Qoran in their hands, swore in the form that I had given."

Though twenty thousand soldiers of Bābur swore on the Qoran to win or die in the battle but not to leave the field alive, yet Bābur was not assured of success, and conscious of the grave consequences of a defeat at this juncture, he renewed[1] the negotiations with the Maharana through Silhiddi, the Chief of Raisen. He offered to make *Peela khal* near Byana the boundary of their respective dominions and give an annual tribute to the Maharana on condition of being left Delhi and its dependencies."[2]

[1] The *Tabqati Akbari* says that at this Council the grandees advised Bābur to retire to the Panjab.

[2] Tod's *Rajasthan*, Vol. I., p. 305: "We can well believe," says he, "that in the position Bābur then was, he would not scruple to promise anything"—p. 306.

The advisers of the Maharana, with whom Silhidi was not at all popular, dissuaded Sāngā from accepting these terms, and the negotiations finally came to an end. Colonel Tod says that though the arrangement was negatived, treason had effected the salvation of Bābur. Silhidi, seeing that though the Maharana had been offered more than what he had started from Chitor to fight for, the overtures were rejected only because he was the medium. He took it to heart and determined to stand in the way of victory.

This ill-advised inactivity of the Maharana while Bābur was cooped up in his encampment, though partly explained by the protracted negotiations for peace made by Bābur, was most deplorable. If he supposed that Bābur was in the toils and that every day's delay brought with it increased danger to him, he should also have considered that delay is always fatal to the cohesion of a heterogenous mass like that by which he was surrounded, all parts of which owned neither the same patriotic feelings by which he was actuated, nor were bound by the same common interest. For the success of the operations of a leader of such a coalition, swift action is a *sine qua non!* Delay gives scope to the play of disruptive forces which bring certain ruin on the whole body. Such forces inhere in composite masess and are only held in check by concentrating the attention of all on one definite aim, by means the most direct and easily understood by all. The Maharana was surrounded by a number of chiefs whose interests never coincided, who came from different provinces, who belonged to different and often hostile communities who even differed in faith, whose aims in life were different and in several instances conflicting; whose only common tie was admiration for and confidence in the heroic personality of the Maharana. In such a situation, the leader to achieve success, must possess energy and courage more than caution and patience; bold aggressiveness more than humanity and forbearance. He must keep the various elements of his army fully employed, and their energies directed to achieving as speedily as possible the common aim. Halting action, faltering attitude, waiting upon time to do the work of the sword are fatal, and entail certain defeat. If the Maharana had possessed the restless energy of his elder brother, the ever-memorable, the "winged" Prithviraj, or if he did possess it, had shown it in a speedy attack on the entrenched camp of Bābur; or if, with Rana Hammir's energy, he had fallen on the dejected, panic-stricken followers of the brave adventurer from Samarkand, the Turk (Moghul) dynasty would probably never have occupied the throne of Delhi,[1] and the history of India would have run a different course from what it has done. The Maharana's delay in coming to an action gave time to Bābur to instil some of his own courage of despair, some of his own heroic ardour into his dejected followers, as well as

[1] Mr. Elphinstone in his *History of India*, page 373, says: "Bābur's advanced guard was immediately attacked; and though reinforced from the main body, was defeated with heavy loss. If the Raja had pressed on during the first panic, *he would have obtained an easy victory*.

to give a start to the disruptive forces in the Maharana's army and set treason to work.

Losing finally all hope of a peaceful settlement with the Maharana, Bābur determined to make the most of his resources and give battle. Taking advantage of the excitement and the exhilaration produced by his appeal to the religion of his followers, and their practical response to it, and in order to keep up their newly-acquired spirit, he broke up the camp to which he had been confined for nearly a month and marched in order of battle to a position two miles in advance. And he had no time to lose. The dangers were thickening around him. "Insurrection and revolt had appeared on every hand. The towns and forts, of which he had gained possession with so much labour, were fast slipping out of his hands. Rābera and Chandwar on the Jumna, Koel (Aligarh) in the Doab, and Sambhal beyond the Ganges, but all of them near Agra, had been retaken by the Afghans.

His troops had been obliged to abandon Kanauj. Gwalior was blockaded by the Rajputs of the vicinity. Alam Khan, who was sent to relieve it, instead of excuting his orders, had marched off to his own country. Many Hindu chiefs had deserted the cause of the emperor. Indeed the previous conquests and present success of Rana Sāngā, had inspired all his countrymen with hopes that a change of dynasty was about to take place."[1]

On the 12th of March, Bābur drew forward his guns and a kind of defensive cover that moved on wheels, and which served as a breast work, supporting them by his matchlocks and all his army. He himself galloped along the line animating his troops and officers and giving them instructions. He threw up other trenches further in advance, near the spot which he fixed upon as favourable for a general action, and when they were finished, advanced

[1] Erskine's *History of India*, Vol. I, p. 469.

to occupy them, dragging forward his guns. As soon as they reached the ground the Rajputs were seen advancing. All were ordered to their posts. Bābur mounted, and drew up his troops, riding cheerfully along the ranks and assuring them of victory. He took the centre to himself, assisted by Chin Timur Sultan. The right wing he committed to Humayun, who had under him Kasim Husain Sultan, Hindu Beg, and Khusrau Kokiltash; the left he entrusted to his son-in-law, Sayad Mehdi Khwaja, and Muhammad Sultan Mirza, Abdul Aziz and Muhammad Ali Jeng-jeng. He appointed strong reserves to carry succour wherever it was required, and on the right and left placed two flanking columns composed of Moghul troops to wheel round the flank and rear of the Rajputs in the heat of the battle on a signal given. This arrangement he had learned in his wars with the Uzbeks. His artillery, under Ustad Ali Kuli, was placed in the centre, in front, connected by chains and protected by movable defences, behind which were placed matchlock men, and in the rear a body of chosen troops ready to repel any attack from behind or to rush forward and charge whenever possible.

The Maharana's army consisted of his own and that of the great chieftains who acknowledged his supremacy or followed his lead. Raja Silhidi, the Rajput Chief of Bhilsa and Raisen, commanded 35,000 horse; Rawal Udai Singh of Dungarpur and Hasan Khan Mewati, 12,000 each; Raja Medni Rai of Chanderi, 10,000 horse; Narbad Hada of Boondi, 7,000; Khinchi Shatrudeva of Gagrone, 6,000; Bhar Mal of Idar, Rao Viramdeva of Merta and Chauhan Narsinghdeva, 4,000 each. Sultan Mahmud Lodi, a son of Sikandar Lodi, commanded 10,000 adventurers; various other chiefs had each from 4,000 to 7,000 men. Rai Mal Rāthor, Commander-in-chief of Jodhpur, and Kanwar Kalyan Mal, heir of Bikaner, commanded 3,000 each. Prithviraj of Amber,[1] Rawat Bagh Singh of Deolia (Pratapgarh),

[1] Many historical records do not mention his presence at the battle.

Chandra Bhan, Manik Chand Chauhan, Rai Dalip and others commanded large divisions.

The battle began about half-past nine in the morning by violent charges made by the Rajputs on Bābur's right and centre, which began to give way. Bodies of the reserve were pushed on to their assistance, and Mustafa Rumi, who commanded one portion of the artillery, opened fire on the masses of Rajput cavalry rushing forward and falling on the Turks like falcons on their prey. This fire made large gaps amongst them; still new bodies of Rajputs pushed on undauntedly. The battle was equally desperate on the left. Just as the Turks began to show signs of wavering, the traitor Silhiddi, who commanded the van (*herole*) of the Maharana's army, went over to Bābur with his 35,000 cavalry. This did not make much difference, but just at that time an arrow discharged by some one struck with such force on the forehead of the Maharana, who was seated on an elephant, as to make him lose consciousness. The chieftains around him considered it advisable to send him out of the battlefield, and appoint a person as his representative, to continue the battle. They placed him in a palanquin and sent him with an escort towards Mewat. They asked Rao Ratan Singh, the chief of Salumbar, to take the Maharana's place and continue the battle. Ratan Singh replied that his ancestor had relinquished the throne of Mewar, which was by right his, and that he would not now accept it even temporarily. He added that he deemed it his duty to serve with zeal whosoever should occupy the royal elephant as the Maharana's representative, and so long as a drop of blood was left in his body, never to allow the enemy to pierce the army under him. Then, Raj Rana Ajjaji, who held the first rank among the nobles of Mewar, and who had, like the great Chonda, out of chivalrous regard for his father's wishes, relinquished his right to the throne of Halvad in Kathiawar in S. 1520 (A.D. 1463), but was adorned with all the ensigns of royalty (of Halvad), was unanimously voted to take the place of the Maharana. And Ajjaji, assuming all the ensigns of the sovereign of Mewar, occupied the vacant seat[1] on the royal elephant. *A chattra* (canopy) was held over him and the *chanwar* was waved over his head. For a little while the Rajputs continued fighting; but the rumour soon spread like wildfire, that the Maharana had been wounded and removed from the field. The bond which had tied the different sections of his forces together was thus broken, and various sections of the Maharana's army, not finding their leader present, left the field.[2] Rawal Udai Singh of Dungarpur, Hasan Khan Mewati, Raja Manik Chand and Chandra Bhan the Chauhan chiefs of Mewar, Rawat Ratan Singh Chondawat of Salumbar, Raj Rana Ajja, Rao Ramdas Sonagarah, Gokal-

[1] A poet says :—

रघु कुलतिलक राण, सिरधारे गजसिर चढे।
काटे खल तुरकाण, ईस जतो किधो अजा ॥

(Assuming on his head the ensigns of the family of Raghu (the great ancestor of Rana, the chief of the Solar dynasty of kings) ascends the elephant : cuts down the wicked Turks, such was the triumph achieved by Ajja).

[2] A bardic song says that the Turks lost 50,000 men in this battle, and that Ajja went to heaven with 9,000 brave Rajputs.

पड़ नर सहस पचास मेछ घण मार न मंडे।
नव सहस समठ लेकर मठर सुरपुर दिशा सिधाविधी ॥

das Parmar, whose descandants hold Bijolian (Mewar), Rai Mal Rathor, heir-apparent of Marwar; the brave Mertia leaders Ratan Singh (the father of the celebrated Miranbai) and Rai Mal, and others were killed after performing deeds of valour.[1]

The Rajputs lost the battle, not because they were inferior to the enemy, but because of one of those chances that have often decided the fate of kingdoms in India, irrespective of the intellectual and material resources of the parties engaged.. It was so with the powerful Raja Anandpal of the Panjab who, in spite of his unquestioned superiority over Sultan Mahmud of Ghazni, lost the famous battle near Peshawar in 1008 A.D. owing to his elephant becoming unruly and turning back in the midst of the battle. It was so again in the case of Dara Shikoh, who was chiefly supported by the Rajputs and who lost the battle of Samugarh in A.D. 1658, owing to his transferring his seat in the

[1] Tod says that Mahmud Lodi was killed in this battle, but Mr. Erskine says that he fled to Gujarat. Mehta Nainsi's *Chronicles* give the date of the battle as Katik Sud 5th, S. 1584.

midst of the battle from the elephant's *howda* to the back of a horse, on the treacherous advice of the traitor, Khalilullah Khan.

That accidents could have such decisive influence on matters of such transcending national importance was due chiefly to the political consciousness of the people having become dormant. *Swadharma,* the duty of the individual to the State, to the nation, to the country in its broadest aspects, had come to mean devotion to the person of the sovereign for the time being and *nothing more.* This contraction of the meaning of the term *Swadharma,* this restrictive application of it accorded with the facts of life in the country, where the rights of the individuals comprising the nation became merged, not in the right of the State as with the military nations of the European continent, but into the will of the person occupying the throne for the time being. The king being the sole arbiter of the destinies of a nation, the only source of power, his personality counted for all *even* in a battle. He being the head—real and not a figurehead only—he won or lost: the nation only because of him. If the arrow had struck Bābur's forehead instead of Sāngā's, the result would have been the same—a complete defeat of the Turks. In fact, in their case, it would have meant annihilation, because of their being foreign interlopers in the country.

The present European War instinctively brings before the mind the great advance the Western nations have achieved in politics during the last four centuries. In Europe every man, woman and child understands his duty to the State, which, he knows, is nothing more than his own individual interest in the higher sense of the term. He or she understands that he or she loses or gains as his or her nation loses or gains, that his or her interests are identical with those of the nation or the State. This spirit animating all, the resources of the whole nation are fully organised and are unhesitatingly employed to protect as well as to promote the cause of the nation or even of individuals, whenever occasion requires. A war in modern times is therefore a war of one nation or a combination of nations against another nation or two or more nations combined. The entire intellectual, moral and material resources of nations are mobilized and used in the struggle. The result is that that belligerent wins whose organisation is superior and whose resources, taken as a whole, are greater than those of the enemy. As a necessary consequence, wars now are immeasurably more devastating, and though both sides are in the end exhausted, the vanquished is the party clearly proved to be the weaker.

This also explains the vast difference that we find between the nature and importance of a battle in those days and a battle in the twentieth century. The battle of Khānua, in which the opposing armies numbered about three lakhs, lasted a few hours, and what momentous issues hung on the result of that battle! It decided the fate of a country inhabited by a fifth part of the human race. It threw back for ever the advancing tide of the triumphant Rajput race, and placed India, with a civilization and culture as old as history and as high as the highest in the world, under the domination of the less civilized Afghans and the highlanders of Central Asia. Compare this with the battles fought in Europe in the great war raging there now. The battle of the Marne lasted four months, and the loss of life in this one battle far exceeded the entire armies engaged in the battle between Bābur and Sāngā; but what is the net result of the victory over the enemy? A few thousand yards of "No Man's Land," with hardly any effect on the final issue of the war.

Victory remained with Bābur, who assumed the title of Ghazi. He advanced to Byana, where he arrived after three days, and held a council of his nobles as to the advisability of following up the victory by an invasion of the Rana's dominions. Bābur's resources, however, were so crippled and the dread of meeting Sāngā in the field a second time was so great, that the approach of the hot season was pleaded as an excuse and the enterprise was given up.[1]

[1] "That Bābur respected and dreaded his foe, we have the best proof in his not risking another battle with him."—Tod's *Rajasthan*, Vol. I, p. 307.

CHAPTER XIV.

"Last Days of Sāngā."

When the party carrying the unconscious Maharana reached Baswa, now the northern boundary of the Jaipur State, the Maharana regained consciousness and at once enquired how the battle had ended. When the whole story was related to him, he became sorrowful, and scolded the people about him for removing him from the field of battle, as that exposed him to the reproach of fleeing from the field. He refused to move towards Chitor, and vowed that he would never enter it alive without vanquishing Bābur.

In consequence of his removal from the battlefield, Sāngā shut himself up for a time in his palace in Ranthambhore. A charan named Todar Mal Chanchlia, who was with the greatest difficulty allowed access to the Maharana by those around him, greeted Sānga with a stirring poem.[1] This shattered the dejection of the Maharana and roused him to action again. The Maharana bestowed the village of Bakan on the charan (which is still in the possession of his descendants), and began to make preparations for resuming hostilities with Bābur.

[1] Apprehending that the charan would stir the Maharana again to take the field against Bābur, those who were in attendance on Sāngā refused the charan entry into the place where the Maharana resided. On this, the charan sat down in front of the palace gate, refused to move from there, and took a vow not to partake of food till he saw the Maharana. He passed three days and nights without food. At last, the ministers, fearing that the charan—whose person according to custom is sacred—would starve himself to death, allowed him to enter the palace and see the Maharana. The charan, as soon as he came near Sāngā, greeted him with the following song composed by himself:—

सतवार जरासिंध आगल श्रीरंग,
विमुहा टीकम दीध वग,
मेलि घात मारे मधुसूदन
असुर घात नांखे अलग ॥ १ ॥

पारथ हेकरसां हथणापुर,
हटियो त्रिया पड़ंता हाथ ॥
देख जका दुरजोधन कीधी,
पछै तका कीधी कांई पाथ ॥ २ ॥

Though the Western Afghan confederacy was crushed by the victory of Khānua, the Eastern confederacy continued to gather strength. The Rajputs though defeated in a great battle, had not been vanquished. Bābur had thus two powerful foes still to overcome before he could consider his throne firmly established. His experience taught him that he had more to fear from the

एकरां राम लयी तिय रावण,
मंद हरेगो दहकमल ॥
डीकम सोहि अपघर मारिया,
जगनायक अपरा जल ॥ ३ ॥

एक राड़ भवमांझ अवट्टयो,
थोरस आये केम उर ॥
मालहतणा केवा कज मांगा,
सांगा तू साले असुर ॥ ४ ॥

(Why this dejection? Sri Krishna had to leave the field a hundred times against Jarasandha: finally after saving himself, he vanquished the enemy. Once Arjuna fell back when Duryodhana cast his hand on Draupadi: all know what Duryodhana did, but you know what Arjuna then did to Duryodhana. Once the foolish ten-headed Ravan took away Sita, but then what did Rama do to him after bridging the sea? Why dost thou take a single defeat to heart like this, oh Sāngā? thou art a thorn in the side of the enemy).

Thakur Bhur Singh of Malsisar in his *Maharana Yash Prakash* (p. 71), says that the charan was Soda Jamnaji.

Rajputs than the Pathans, and he resolved to break the power of the Rajput kings by attacking them one by one before they might combine again and wrest his hard-won throne from him. He left the Eastern Afghan confederacy to itself for a while, little suspecting that it would, after his death, overwhelm his son and successor and drive him out of India, and would be finally crushed only with the help of the Rajputs by his grandson Akbar.

Being rightly afraid of the great power of the Rajput kings of the west, Bābur resolved to attack Raja Medni Rai of Chanderi, one of the bravest and ablest of the Maharana's lieutenants. Leaving Agra in December 1527 A.D., he arrived at Kalpi on 1st January, A.D. 1528, and passing by Irej (Irich) and Kechwa, reached Chanderi on the 20th of the month. Sāngā, hearing that Bābur had gone towards Chanderi, marched to attack him and arrived at Irich. But here his ministers, who were opposed to further warfare, finding the war-like Maharana bent on plunging into war again, administered poison to him. The heroic spirit of the great man would not so easily give in, and fought with the malady for a time. At last the poison prevailed and Sāngā breathed his last at Baswa in Baisakh[1] Sud, S. 1584, after a reign of 21 years 5 months and 9 days. Thus ended the glorious life of the great man who was one of the greatest sovereigns that have ever ruled in Rajputana. The lesser men who were about him in his last days, purchased "by regicide, inglorious ease and safety, in preference to privations and dangers, and to emulating the manly constancy of their prince, who resolved to make heavens his canopy till his foe was crushed,—a determination which was pursued with the most resolute perseverance by some of his gallant successors."[2]

Maharana Sāngā was of middle stature but of great muscular strength, fair in complexion, with unusually large eyes. He

[1] *Chaturkula Charitra* p. 27 gives the date as Magh Sud 9th, S. 1584.

[2] Tod's *Rajasthan*, Vol. I, p. 307.

exhibited at his death, "but the fragments of a warrior; one eye was lost in the broil with his brother (Prithviraj), an arm in an action with the Lodi King of Delhi, and he was a cripple owing to a limb being broken by a cannon ball in another, while he counted eighty wounds from the sword or the lance on various parts of his body. He was celebrated for energetic enterprise, of which his capture of Mahmud, King of Malwa, in his own capital is a celebrated instance; and his successful storming of the almost impregnable Ranthambhore, though ably defended by the imperial general Ali, gained him great renown. Had he been succeeded by a prince possessed of his foresight and judgment, Bābur's descendants might not have retained the sovereignty of India."[1]

Tod's *Rajasthan*, Vol. I, pp. 307, 308.

INDEX.